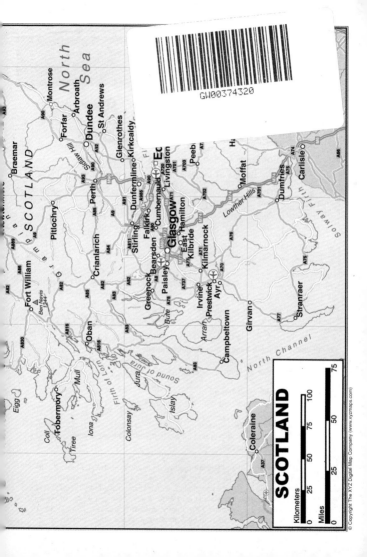

GW00374320

SCOTLAND

Kilometers
0   25   50   75   100

Miles
0   25   50   75

Buytel™

FREE Calls &
Save up to 88%

Compare to see how much you can save:

Calling From UK	Using a BT Landline			Using a BT Pay Phone		
	Travel Card	Direct Dial	Savings on 10min call	Travel Card	Direct Dial	Savings on 10min call
Ireland	7p	23p	£1.60 (70%)	25p	66p	£4.10 (62%)
France	7p	28p	£2.10 (75%)	25p	66p	£4.10 (62%)
Germany	7p	28p	£2.10 (75%)	25p	66p	£4.10 (62%)
Italy	7p	36p	£2.90 (81%)	25p	75p	£5.00 (67%)
US	7p	24p	£1.70 (71%)	25p	75p	£5.00 (67%)
Malaysia	8p	67p	£5.90 (88%)	26p	150p	£12.40 (83%)

All rates are per minute for a weekday, daytime call, from a
landline using freephone access, to a landline and include taxes.
Rates correct at 01/08/04.

Secured By
Voice *vault*
TM

20 minutes FREE international calls from any phone
Scratch off the PIN on the front of the Travel Card, dial an access number,
register and make 20 minutes of FREE* calls.

Get £3.50 FREE when you top-up
If you enter your credit card details when you enrol.

Get 100 FREE game credits
If you quote the PIN on this Travel Card when you purchase a game. For more
details, see www.buytel.com.

★ Free calls are to landlines in any Ryanair destination country, Australia, China, North
America, South Africa or Russia. Subsequent calls, mobile calls or calls outside these
destinations will be charged at the prevailing rate detailed on www.buytel.com. Free calls
may be for one or a number of calls and is valid for 5 days from enrolment. Offers valid
for registrations before 1st December 2004, limited to MasterCard, Visa, Laser or Switch
Card holders and may not be used with other promotions unless otherwise stated.

CALL FREE*

to any landline in a Ryanair destination country, Australia, China, North America, South Afric… … Russia with this Travel Card

Massive savin… … all your calls!

CALL: +35… 1 2462366

and we will call you back within 15 seconds
with a line for you to make your call!

Buytel™

TRAVEL TIPS - easy ways to make the same call for less!

CALLING FROM A LAND LINE:
Avoid exorbitant hotel and pay phone charges by using a Buytel local access number, free phone number or by requesting a call back. It's simple to use!

CALLING FROM A MOBILE PHONE (CELLPHONE):
Don't use your home mobile when travelling as operators apply outrageous roaming charges to every call made or received outside their home territory.

If you must use your home mobile, then only use it for text messages but again the operators charge more for international SMS than local SMS.

Buytel Eurofone

Most seasoned travellers find a local solution. They purchase a local SIM or a **Eurofone** (available from www.buytel.com) which works in over 80 countries. There are no surprises with the **Eurofone** as you only pay for the calls you use and you may top-up anytime, anywhere! In addition, you may forward your home numbers to the **Eurofone** so that you never miss a call.

Eurofone is available online at www.buytel.com or as an option to registered Travel Card customers.

Buytel also delivers direct to your door - if you are in any European city, delivery is usually within 48 hours of order. Contact us on www.buytel.com or call +353 1 246 2332.

Scotland

Text: Robin Gauldie

Text editors: Joanne O'Reilly & Anna Brosnan

Cartography: Global Mapping Ltd

Advertising: Contact Publicity

Design: Suzanne Murray

Production: Mark Webster

Photography: Scottish Viewpoint Picture Library
www.scottishviewpoint.com

Publishing Information:
This edition was first published in 2004
by Premier Guides Ltd., Envision House, Flood St., Galway.
Email: info@premierguides.net
Dublin Office: Email: info@selectmedialtd.com

Publishers: Denis Lane & Robert Heuston

Typeset in Meta and ATRotis Serif 55
ISBN: 1-904895-06-9
Printed in Ireland

Premier Guides Ltd

© Premier Guides Ltd 2004

If you have any questions, queries or suggestions we'd be delighted to hear your
contributions for the next edition. Please send to updates@premierguides.net

INSIDE THIS EDITION

Scotland.
Welcome to our life.

The No.1 booking and information service for Scotland: www.visitscotland.com

Register online for a free information pack in your language! While you're in Scotland, call 0845 22 55 121 or visit our tourist information centres to book-a-bed-ahead!

Scotland

Enjoying Scotland so much
you want to stay?

Why not extend your time in Scotland and maybe visit some attractions shown in this guide. Now Ryanair have made it easier and cheaper for their customers to change their reservations. You can now retrieve and change the time and date of your flight on www.ryanair.com or through our reservation centre.

You can change your booking online up to 12 hours prior to scheduled departure subject to availability. Between 12 and 3 hours prior to your scheduled departure you can change your booking by contacting your local Ryanair reservations centre, subject to call centre opening hours. Ryanair's UK reservation number is shown below. For details and costs associated with changing your reservation please check out our website or simply talk to one of our reservation agents on the number below.

Contacting Ryanair:

UK Reservations Number: 0871 246 0000*
*Can only be called when in the UK (10p per minute)

Opening Hours:
Monday - Friday 09.00 - 17.45
Saturday 09.00 - 17.45
Sunday 10.00 - 17.45

Further European contact numbers can be located at
www.ryanair.com

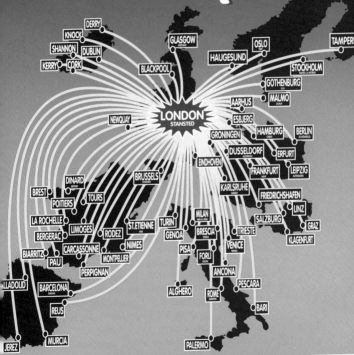

For its small size, Scotland is one of the world's best-loved travel destinations, attracting a wide variety of visitors with its potent mixture of romantic history, stunning mountain and island scenery, cutting-edge culture and vibrant urban life.

Few small countries can match its diversity and part of Scotland's appeal is that so much can be packed into a short holiday. The beautiful countryside of the Trossachs and Loch Lomond, the moors and glens of Perthshire or Argyll and the castles and historic towns of Lothian and the Borders are all within a couple of hours drive of Glasgow or Edinburgh. Even its Western Isles are easily reached by ferry, road or air.

Scotland has a complex and fascinating history, which can be explored on the ground or in the array of world-class museums and purpose-built visitor centres. Picts, Scots, Vikings and Normans have all left their mark on a distinctive national culture that has flourished in the aftermath of devolution. Part of that history has been their struggle for independence and the creation of a national parliament has given the Scots a large measure of control over their own political destiny.

Scotland's cities – especially Glasgow and Edinburgh, its two most important gateways – have a worldwide tourism profile that attracts everyone from back-packers, drawn by its vibrant nightlife, to those in search of their Scottish roots, to admirers of Scotland's writers, poets and artists, to ghost-hunters and gourmands. Out of town, but not too far, there are gaunt North Sea cliffs topped by ruined castles, craggy isles teeming with seabirds, and sweeping stretches of empty, breathtaking Atlantic and Irish Sea coastlines.

Calton Hill with
a view towards
the Edinburgh
skyline

There's a huge array of sports and activities waiting to be discovered, from the world's most revered golf courses to football (for Scotland has always been football crazy), to some of the best trout and salmon fishing in the world, hill walking and mountaineering, along with more modern adrenaline sports.

Then there are the people: with a dozen or more regional identities that go to make up the nation, from Gaelic-speaking Hebrideans to the streetwise citizens of Glasgow.

Since the setting up of the Scottish Parliament five years ago, Scotland has found a new self-confidence. Even before that, Glasgow's ego had been boosted when it won the right to be a European Cultural City and the slogan 'Glasgow's Miles Better' helped the city hoist itself by its bootlaces out of a long depression.

A healthy rivalry between Edinburgh – Scotland's capital – and Glasgow, its biggest city and industrial centre, has ensured that visitors will find an ever-increasing range of attractions and accommodation in both cities.

The remains of Arbroath Abbey- a Tironensian Monastery

Until 1997, when the first Labour government in eighteen years came to power, Scotland's political centre of gravity lay well to the left and Scots felt increasingly isolated and disenfranchised from a London government, which ignored their needs and desires. The political landscape changed for the better with the landslide that wiped the Tories from the face of Scotland, but unemployment remains an issue in rural and urban communities.

North Sea oil reserves, which could have been an engine of economic development and national regeneration, were mostly squandered during the 1980s and 1990s to underwrite the 'Thatcher revolution' in England. Despite some new finds, North Sea oil is close to running out and fishing, one of the last of Scotland's traditional industries, is near to terminal decline.

New industries are being developed to replace the old and Scotland has cultivated centres of excellence across a range of sectors. International call-centres have become major employers and biotechnology is thriving. Dundee – still the home of some of Britain's best-loved comic-strip characters such as Desperate Dan and Dennis the Menace – is a world leader in video-game creation. Glasgow and Edinburgh are major financial and new-technology centres, and tourism is a more important part of Scotland's economy than ever before.

Scotland is a small country that is easily explored. Glasgow and Edinburgh lie less than 60 miles apart – Glasgow on the Clyde, Edinburgh on the Firth of Forth,

Looking down towards the bridge at the Falls of Dochart

within sight of the North Sea. Perth is only 60 miles from both Glasgow and Edinburgh, and Inverness, gateway to the Highlands, is around 120 miles away.

South of the narrow isthmus between Forth and Clyde, where the Romans built Antonine's Wall to keep the fierce Picts at bay and where some of the bloodiest battles in Scotland's turbulent history have been fought, lie the rolling hills of Lothian and the Borders. To the north is the gentle highland countryside of the Trossachs, and still further north is the increasingly dramatic scenery of Argyll, Perthshire, the Grampian mountains and the northern Highlands.

Don't come to Scotland expecting Mediterranean weather. But, as they say, there's no such thing as bad weather – just the wrong clothes. Whatever time of year you visit Scotland you can expect to experience a taste of all four seasons.

GLASGOW. **THE NEW BLACK.**

SEDUCTIVE SHOPPING. ACHINGLY HIP HOTELS. ICE-COOL WATERING HOLES. AND SOME SERIOUSLY ROMANTIC ART NOUVEAU ARCHITECTURE COURTESY OF CHARLES RENNIE MACKINTOSH.

FOR A LONG, LUXURIOUS WEEKEND IN A CITY THAT'S NOT SHORT ON STYLE, THERE IS ONLY ONE LABEL TO LUST AFTER.

IT'S CALLED GLASGOW.

WWW.SEEGLASGOW.COM

Currency and Banking

The currency is the pound sterling (£), which is issued in notes of £5, £10, £20, £50 and £100 and in coins of £1, £2 and 1p, 2p, 5p, 10p, 20p, 50p. In addition to notes issued by the Bank of England (the British national bank), Scottish notes are also issued by the Bank of Scotland, Royal Bank of Scotland and Clydesdale Bank. Although these are valid currency throughout the UK, they can sometimes be difficult to spend or exchange outside Scotland.

Banks are open 09.30-15.30 Monday-Friday. Bureaux de change at airports and in Edinburgh city centre stay open longer, and there are plenty of automatic teller machines (ATMs), which accept all major debit and credit cards bearing the Cirrus or Maestro symbols. Credit and debit cards are accepted in shops, bars, pubs, hotels and restaurants almost everywhere, though smaller bed-and-breakfast guesthouses and rural pubs and cafés may prefer to be paid in cash.

Tipping is at the discretion of the customer, but is increasingly common in smarter bars and cafés as well as in up-market restaurants.

Central Station, Glasgow, built for Caledonian Railway and opened in 1879

Transport

In Glasgow, the Strathclyde Passenger Transport (SPT) Subway is modern, fast and reliable, with trains every four minutes at peak times, calling at each of the fifteen stations on the double circular route north and south of the river. There are park and ride facilities at four of the stations, and direct links to the national rail network at Partick and Buchanan Street stations. Outer suburbs are linked to the centre by an over-ground suburban rail system.

Ryanair have flights into Scotland's key airports. Aberdeen International Airport, is Scotland's most northerly airport and is also home to an important helicopter base. Edinburgh Airport is conveniently located in the heart of Scotland within easy reach of Fife, Aberdeenshire and Tayside. Glasgow Prestwick International is Ryanair's gateway to western Scotland. Glasgow Prestwick International, is the only airport in Scotland served by

The harbour of Lerwick

its own railway station, not far from the check-in desks, and connected to the terminal by an enclosed skywalk. ScotRail trains connect the airport with Glasgow, Ayr and other points between 06.00 and 23.08, and the X99 bus service links the airport with Glasgow Buchanan Street Station from 23.00-06.00. The airport is also connected to central Glasgow by frequent shuttle buses operated by Dodds of Troon. The city bus network is comprehensive, and taxis are plentiful and relatively cheap. They can be hailed on the street or found at taxi ranks at the airport and main city centre railway stations.

Rail services operated by Scotrail, Virgin Trains and GNER connect Scotland's two major cities with each other and with Stirling, Perth, Inverness, Dundee and Aberdeen and smaller towns en route between these cities. Flights from Glasgow, and Caledonian MacBrayne ferries from Oban and Mallaig, link the Western Isles with the mainland, and a controversial new road bridge has replaced the ferry to the Isle of Skye.

Coach tour company Dodds of Troon offers a wide range of five-day package holidays around Scotland, with hotels in the Western Highlands and Skye, Dunoon on the Clyde coast and Crieff in Perthshire.

Motorways connect Glasgow, Edinburgh, Perth and Inverness, with a dual carriageway link between Perth and Dundee. North of Inverness roads are narrower and in the remote Highlands may even be single-track.

In a peaceful corner of South-west Scotland stands a towering castle...

And surrounding the towering castle is an enormous country park...

...And in the enormous country park are some tall, tall trees...

And in those tall, tall trees hide some shy little red squirrels...

And seeing one of those shy little red squirrels is the thing my sister liked best about her day out at Culzean.

— *Culzean Castle & Country Park* —

Visit the magnificent Culzean Castle and you'll find something the whole family will enjoy. So for a big, big day out call **(01655) 884455** or visit **www.nts.org.uk** for opening times and details of our special events.

The National Trust
for Scotland

For you.

GLASGOW

Glasgow is Scotland's largest city and the heart of a sprawling conurbation that is home to around one million people (almost one fifth of the country's total population). Glasgow nightlife rocks; its pubs and bars are second to none and it is the birthplace of some of Britain's top music names. It is home to the 'Old Firm' of Glasgow Celtic and Glasgow Rangers, traditionally Scotland's leading football teams, and to **Hampden Park**, the national stadium, which now houses a major-league football museum.

Glasgow is also a hub of high culture. The **Scottish Opera**, the **Scottish Royal Ballet**, and the renowned **Glasgow School of Art**, which has fostered some of Scotland's greatest artistic talents, can all be found here. As well as being a hothouse for the arts, it's the heart of Scotland's TV, cinema and media scene.

Gordon Street (outside Central Station), Glasgow

Though founded in the Middle Ages, Glasgow's industrial and commercial fortunes were made in the nineteenth century. The jewels of its architectural heritage, such as the central **Merchant City district**, now a rejuvenated area of trendy shops, bars and apartments, date from this Victorian golden age.

George Square, in the city centre, is a handy point to start exploring Glasgow, and is overlooked by the

Old and new buildings on the corner of Robertson Street and Broomielaw

mock-Renaissance **City Chambers** – the meeting place of the city council. **Sauchiehall Street**, the city's main shopping artery, is a short walk from the square. Further west, **Byres Road**, close to Glasgow University, is a lively hub for youthful nightlife with numerous bars and clubs catering to the city's large student population.

The **Glasgow Science Centre**, with cutting-edge interactive exhibits and a 120-seat planetarium, is one of the city's newest attractions. Opposite it, moored on the north bank of the River Clyde, is the **Tall Ship** at Glasgow Harbour. Built in 1896, the sailing ship *Glenlee* was one of the last such vessels to be built in the Clyde shipyards.

Another twenty-first century addition to Glasgow's array of attractions is the **Scottish Museum of Football** at Hampden Park, Scotland's national football stadium, about five miles south of the city centre. Opened in 2000, the Museum of Football celebrates the nation's greatest players and their achievements on the national and international scene. It houses a fascinating collection of photos and soccer memorabilia.

Another of the city's main attractions is the **Kelvingrove Art Gallery and Museum**, which includes an impressive collection of works by French impressionist painters and the Burrell Collection, an eclectic array of paintings and objets d'art. On the University of Glasgow campus, the **Hunterian Museum and Art Gallery**, the oldest in Scotland, has an excellent collection of archaeological finds and works by Scottish artists. Worth seeing is the **House for an Art Lover** at Bellahouston Park, which was designed by the renowned Glaswegian architect and interior designer Charles Rennie Mackintosh. **The People's Palace** at Glasgow Green and the **Tenement House** at 145 Buccleuch Street are fascinating exhibitions of working class life in nineteenth-century Glasgow.

For bargains galore, head for the **Barras**. This covered market near Glasgow Cross has been selling an amazing variety of bargains for more than a hundred years, with more than 800 shops and stalls selling second-hand clothing, antiques, records, CDs and even live pets.

River Clyde crossed by Bell's footbridge to the Armadillo

AYRSHIRE

One of Scotland's most famous sons, the poet Robert Burns (1759-96), author of 'Tam O'Shanter', 'A Man's a Man for a' that' and many more poems and ballads, is responsible for placing Ayrshire firmly on the tourist map. While its world-class greens of Troon (a haven for golfers), keep it there.

Loch Green golf course at Troon, Firth of Clyde, South Ayrshire

The 'Burns Country', southwest of Glasgow and the Clyde, attracts a steady flow of visitors keen to tread in their hero's footsteps. The poet's birthplace in the **Burns Cottage** at Alloway – just south of Ayr, the county town – is now a museum housing a collection of original manuscripts by Burns. The next-door **Burns Monument**, built in 1823, houses more mementos. At Kirkoswald, **Souter Johnnie's Cottage** was the home of Burns' drinking buddy John Davidson, the village shoemaker and model for Souter Johnnie, Tam O'Shanter's 'honest, drouthy crony' in the famous ballad.

Still more fascinating 'Burnsiana' is to be found at the **Burns House Museum** on Mauchline's Castle Street, which is housed in a cottage the poet rented for Jean Armour, his fiancée, in 1788. Life-size, animated models of Burns and Jean tell their story on the upper floor of the cottage, which is furnished and decorated as it would have been in their time.

Welcome to Prestwick

gateway to

Ayrshire &
the Isle of Arran

more

romance, excitement, activities
relaxation, short breaks...

...**STAY** and enjoy great offers.

www.ayrshire-arran.com
or call **+44 (0)1292 474297**

Ayrshire
&Arran
TOURIST BOARD

"The Big Idea" centre - a hands on exhibition centre, Irvine, North Ayrshire

Mauchline, a small town built around a fifteenth century castle, is known for the decorated wooden boxes called 'Mauchline ware', which today are much sought after by collectors. The town's museum has a great collection.

In **Kilmarnock** the **Loudoun Castle** has all the historical and mythical stories that attach themselves to ancient ruins, however, this is a castle with a difference, it's a theme park wonderland and a fun day out for the family.

Ayrshire's coastline, with its sandy beaches and dramatic scenery, also attracts many visitors. At Irvine, the **Scottish Maritime Museum** features old-fashioned fishing and cargo vessels including a lifeboat, a tug, and one of the nineteenth century 'puffer' steamships that plied their trade up and down the Clyde coast.

At Dalry Road in Kilwinning, the **Dalgarven Mill Ayrshire Museum of Country Life and Costume** is housed in a working watermill, which is more than 400 years old. There are walks along the river, and an extensive collection of tools, furniture and costumes give an insight into the lives of Scottish villagers in centuries past. A bakehouse sells freshly-baked bread made from the mill's own flour.

There's more history at **Vikingar!**, an exciting multimedia attraction at Largs, inspired by the Scots' victory over invading Norsemen at the Battle of Largs in 1263.

Culzean (pronounced 'Cullane') **Castle**, at Maybole village, 12 miles south of Ayr and in the midst of Scotland's oldest country park, is an excellent example of eighteenth-century baronial architecture. Designed by the architect Robert Adam – planner of Edinburgh's gracious New Town district – this castle was built between 1772 and 1792 for the tenth Earl of Cassilis. Dramatically perched on a crag above the sea, it is surrounded by country walks and woods where herds of deer roam.

Culzean Castle, West of Maybole, South Ayrshire

Not far off the Ayrshire coast lies **Arran**, one of Scotland's most dramatic yet most accessible islands. Ferries connect its little port of Brodick with Ardrossan, on the mainland. The island's biggest historic attraction is **Brodick Castle**, where a stately Victorian wing adjoins a thirteenth-century keep. Holidaymakers will find plenty to do on Arran; there are fantastic views of the Clyde Coast from the 2,866 ft summit of **Goatfell** and 2,618 ft **Cir Mhor**, sandy beaches, good sea fishing and birdwatching.

The town of Dumfries

GALLOWAY AND DUMFRIES

The rich, rolling farmland of Galloway has close associations with Robert Burns, who worked as a ploughman in its green fields before becoming a celebrated bard. Galloway faces south across the Solway Firth to England, and Gretna Green, just inside the Scottish border. It once attracted romantic runaways who could not marry in England without the permission of the bride's father. Such permission wasn't needed in Scotland, and eloping couples were traditionally married in the **Old Blacksmith's Shop** with the anvil for an alter. It's now a museum, and Gretna is still a popular place to tie the knot.

Lying so close to the border, the region has a turbulent past and many historic castles and keeps. For example, the impressive battlements of **Caerlaverock Castle**, built in the thirteenth century, are a testament to the powerful border clan, the Maxwells.

Dumfries is a thriving market town on the banks of the river Nith. It is the last point on the Burns' pilgrimage trail, for it is here that the poet is buried, in St Michael's Churchyard. Burns spent the last three years of his short life here, and some of his books and manuscripts are housed in the unassuming **Burns House**, on Burns Street.

The southwest has its whisky trail, too. On the banks of the River Bladnoch near Wigtown, the **Bladnoch Distillery** was founded in 1817. Recently reopened as a visitor centre, with distillery tours, whisky tastings, and one of the best gift shops in the area, its single malts have earned their reputation.

Wigtown, on its south-facing bay, is Scotland's 'Book Town', with more second-hand and antiquarian booksellers than any Scottish city and an annual calendar of readings, book signings and literary events.

Glendarroch Loch, Dumfries & Galloway

Campbeltown, the chief town and port of Kintyre

ARGYLL

Argyll begins on the north shore of the Firth of Clyde and its scenery steadily grows more impressive as you head north. This beautiful region of moors, glens and long, narrow sea-lochs divides the landscape into a series of hilly, heather-covered peninsulas. The most famous of these, immortalised by ex-Beatle Paul McCartney, is the **Mull of Kintyre**, a craggy peninsula that shelters the Firth of Clyde from the open waters of the Irish Sea.

Apart from Beatle fans hoping for a glimpse of their hero (who still lives there) the Mull of Kintyre's beautiful scenery gets remarkably little attention from visitors to Scotland. Its main settlement, **Campbeltown**, is both charming and tranquil.

The little port of **Tarbert**, on the isthmus of the Mull, is the gateway to the Western Isles of Islay and Jura, famed for their malt whiskies. There's more whisky at **Oban**, with its 200-year-old distillery. This cheerful little fishing port offers passage to Mull and the remote Outer Hebrides.

Argyll is the homeland of the Clan Campbell, whose canny chieftains became powerful at the expense of their neighbours by making common cause with the government in Edinburgh and London against the rebellious clans of the north.

Inveraray Castle, the seat of the Duke of Argyll, is a magnificent testament to the power and prestige of the Campbell Clan. **Inveraray Jail** on Church Square in the centre of Inveraray, and the ghostly **Glen Coe,** further north, where in 1692 Campbell soldiers massacred men, women and children of the Macdonald clan, paint a lurid picture of what it was like to be on the receiving end of Campbell justice.

Inveraray sits on the north side of **Loch Fyne,** which is famed for its superb seafood, including some of the world's best kippers (smoked herring) and fresh oysters which are farmed in its clear, cold waters. From Taynuilt, you can take a cruise on the 20-mile-long **Loch Etive,** one of Scotland's loveliest sea-lochs and home to seals, deer, and golden eagles. From Oban, **Loch Linnhe** stretches north to Fort William, the Great Glen and its chain of lochs, which reach across to Inverness and the towering summit of **Ben Nevis.** At 4,406 ft Ben Nevis is the highest peak in Great Britain and Ireland.

Fort William is a good base for exploring this spectacular region, which is scattered with visitor attractions such as the **Ben Nevis Distillery and Visitor Centre** at Lochy Bridge and the **West Highland Museum,** which has a colourful array of clan tartans, fierce-looking Highland weaponry, and Jacobite relics. If the scenery around these parts looks familiar, it's because two of the biggest tartan blockbusters of recent years, *Braveheart*, starring Mel Gibson, and *Rob Roy*, starring Liam Neeson, were both filmed on location around Glen Nevis.

WESTERN ISLES

Wild, remote and underpopulated, the Western Isles rank among the world's most beautiful landscapes, with sweeps of empty white sand beaches and treeless heather moors. In summer the machair, or grassy shoreline, is a blaze of colourful wildflowers, and each island has its own character.

Bowmore Distillery, Islay

Islay and Jura, the furthest south of the Hebridean Isles, are easily accessible, with the five-mile-wide Sound of Jura separating them from the mainland and frequent ferries from Oban and Tarbert. On Islay, the **Bowmore Distillery** is the main visitor attraction, and on Jura, the **Jura House Walled Garden's** lush growth testifies to the warming influence of the Gulf Stream. Even more accessible is **Skye**, probably the best known of all the Scottish isles and linked to the mainland by a road bridge. Here, the main attraction is brooding **Dunvegan Castle**, the seat of the chiefs of Clan Macleod for more than seven centuries. Also worth a visit is the **Museum of the Isles** in the ruined **Armadale Castle**, which tells the story of the Macdonald Lords of the Isles.

Mull, at the mouth of Loch Linnhe and only six miles west of Oban, is the homeland of the Maclean clan. **Duart Castle**, seat of their clan chiefs, is open to visitors. The tiny island of **Iona**, only a short distance off the western tip of Mull, was the birthplace of Christianity in Scotland and was the burial place of Scottish kings for centuries. It has been the home of a religious community since 563 AD when the Irish Saint Columba established a mission here. The Iona Community has restored the mission's oldest surviving building, St Oran's Chapel, built in 1080.

Between Skye and Mull, four tiny, tranquil islands – **Canna**, **Eigg**, **Muck** and **Rhum** – are inhabited by seals and seabirds.

Lewis, the largest of the Western Isles, is almost 60 miles long and its capital, **Stornoway**, is a 65-mile ferry ride from Ullapool, on the Scottish mainland. Low-lying and covered with small lochs, Lewis can be stunningly beautiful in high summer. Among its points of interest are mysterious stone age relics older than the

Isle of Lewis, Outer Hebrides

Pyramids, such as the rings of standing stones at **Callanish** and **Steinacleit**. At **Dun Carloway**, an Iron Age Broch or stone tower is a relic of a slightly more recent era – it is a mere 2,000 years old – and at **Gearannan Village** a collection of the turf walled 'black houses' lived in by Hebrideans, until less than a century ago, has been preserved as a living museum.

River Leven, at Balloch near the marina at the south end of Loch Lomond, West Dunbartonshire

LOCH LOMOND

Scotland's biggest city is close to some of its most beautiful scenery. In few European countries can you travel so quickly from bright city lights to wide open country. Immortalised in song, the bonnie banks of **Loch Lomond** are a mere ten miles from Glasgow's outer suburbs, but the countryside surrounding the peaceful loch, which is the largest body of fresh water in Britain, gives no hint of the busy city nearby. Instead, the loch, which is overlooked by **Ben Lomond**, is surrounded by gentle hills, lush woodland and is dotted with more than a dozen little islands where waterfowl nest.

Loch Lomond connects the rugged country of northern Argyll and the gentler landscapes of central Scotland.

Hugging the west shore of the lake, the A82 highway provides a picturesque drive through the small lakeside villages of **Luss**, **Tarbet** and **Ardlui**. At the narrow northern end of the loch, the scenery becomes increasingly dramatic, with steep hillsides looming over the dark, clear water.

A more relaxing way to see the region's beautiful scenery is to take a daytrip on a cruise boat for a close-up view of the islands. **Balloch**, at the loch's southern end, is the main jumping-off point for Loch Lomond cruising, but some boats also operate from **Balmaha**, on the eastern shore of the loch.

Balloch Castle Country Park, encircling Balloch Castle, offers 200 acres of forest, field and ornamental gardens close to the shores of the loch. A visitor centre within the castle recounts the history of the edifice, its grounds and their surroundings, and Loch Lomond park rangers lead guided walks and tours. The castle has a souvenir shop, café and picnic and barbecue sites.

Each of the loch's islands has its own story to tell. Two – **Bucinch** and **Ceardach** – belong to the National Trust for Scotland and are open year round. On **Inchmurrin**, the spooky ruin of **Lennox Castle** stands on a lakeside hilltop. **Inchcailloch**, which means 'island of the old women', gets its name from the medieval nunnery that once stood there and is the ancient burial-ground of the Macgregor chieftains. The yew trees on **Inchlonaig** are said to have been planted by Robert the Bruce to supply wood for the longbows of his army's archers.

Loch Lomond is a popular summer getaway for Scottish city dwellers, with a range of water sports on offer, including water skiing, dinghy and yacht sailing. There are several good golf courses nearby, along with a range of quality accommodation.

THE TROSSACHS

Between Loch Lomond and the Firth of Forth lies the pocket wilderness of the **Trossachs**, a region of rolling highlands, lochs, moors and woodland, much of which is now embraced by the **Loch Lomond and the Trossachs National Park**, which was designated in 2002.

Britain's newest national park covers four distinct regions, from the slopes of Ben Lomond, overlooking the loch, through the glens and tarns of the Trossachs between **Callander** and **Aberfoyle**, to the high country of **Arrochar**, **Breadalbane** and the **Cowal peninsula**.

Summit of Ben An with a view over Loch Katrine, the Trossachs

This is the homeland of the outlawed Macgregor clan and its most famous son, the bandit and cattle-thief **Rob Roy**, whose story was turned into a romantic legend by the nineteenth-century author Sir Walter Scott. **The Rob Roy and Trossachs Visitor Centre** at Ancaster Square, in the centre of Callander, recounts the true history of the famous outlaw's life.

On a clear day, the slopes of the Trossachs are tantalisingly visible from Edinburgh, promising an escape from the crowded city streets. The region is equally accessible from Glasgow. Both cities are about an hour away by road or rail.

If you only have time for a short break in Glasgow or Edinburgh, yet want to savour some of the wilderness countryside that makes Scotland so special, a day out in the Trossachs is the perfect mini-adventure.

The National Park is a year-round family attraction, with plenty of undemanding walking trails and breathtaking scenery. If you plan to venture into its wilder regions, however, you will need good walking boots, waterproof clothing and a reliable map. Balloch, on the shores of Loch Lomond, provides the western entrée to the National Park, while the market town of Callander is the main gateway to the Trossachs from the east.

In Balloch, the **National Park Gateway Centre** includes a tourist information centre and a state-of-the-art interpretation centre exploring the nature, geology and social history of the Trossachs. Around it is a woodland area graced by artworks commissioned by the Scottish Arts Council. It is a great spot for families, with free activities throughout the year and guided walks led by park rangers.

In the foothills of the Trossachs, at **Killearn** in the Campsie Fells, the **Glengoyne Distillery** is one of the few distilleries still making distinctive single malt whiskies in this part of Scotland. Opened in 1833 and in business ever since, Glengoyne draws its water from a 50-ft waterfall and offers visitors a conducted tour with a taste of its fine malts in a reception room overlooking the glen and the falls.

STIRLING

Straddling the main route between the Highlands and Lowlands, **Stirling** is situated midway between Glasgow and Edinburgh. Its strategic position has meant it has been at the heart of Scotland's troubled history since the earliest times. A cliff top castle dominates the town and overlooks the battlefields where the armies of Wallace and the Bruce defeated the English invaders during the thirteenth and fourteenth century wars of independence. Standing near the head waters of the Forth, Stirling is surrounded by fertile farmland, but not far to the north are dramatic hillsides and empty moorland.

Below the town, **Stirling Old Bridge**, built at the beginning of the fifteenth century, was for hundreds of years the lowest point at which the river could be crossed, except by boat, and is the location of an English defeat at the hands of William Wallace in 1297.

Stirling, a tourist and commercial centre on the south bank of the River Forth

Built around a 250-ft crag that makes it a natural fortress, Stirling is dominated by its castle, which was often home to Scottish monarchs when Edinburgh was held by the English. James II was born in **Stirling Castle**, James IV added tall towers to its defences, James V built a fine Renaissance palace within the walls, and both the tragic Mary, Queen of Scots and her son and heir James VI, spent several years here. Inside the walls is the **Regimental**

Museum of the Argyll and Sutherland Highlanders, the oldest of Scotland's kilted regiments – all of which now appear doomed by plans to modernise the British Army. A sixteenth-century royal chapel and hall are among the castle's more striking aspects.

Next to Stirling Castle, on Castle Hill, a **Visitor Centre** recounts its heritage with an audio-visual display that is a good introduction before entering the castle. **Argyll's Lodging,** opposite the Castle, is a fine, refurbished seventeenth-century building that was formerly the home

Stirling Castle, dating from medieval times

of the Earl of Stirling. Opposite (on Castle Wynd) is **Stirling Old Town Jail,** where you can visit the old cells and shudder at grim leg-irons and handcuffs.

Just outside Stirling, **Bannockburn Heritage Centre** (two miles from the town centre) stands close to the site of Robert the Bruce's decisive victory over the forces of Edward II of England in 1314 and tells the stories of Bruce, the battle and Scotland's long struggle for freedom.

Around Stirling, other sites worth a visit include the picturesque ruins of **Castle Campbell,** a fifteenth-century fortress in Dollar Glen, about ten miles from Stirling, and **Doune Castle,** about eight miles north of the town on the very edge of the Highlands.

LISTINGS

GLENGOYNE DISTILLERY
Dumgoyne, G63 9LB,
Scotland
Tel: 01360 550254
Fax: 01360 550094
Email: reception@glengoyne.com
Web: www.glengoyne.com

Visit 'Scotland's Most Beautfiul Distillery' for guided tours, tastings and our superb whisky shop. Close to Loch Lomond, Glengoyne Distillery is situated on the scenic A81 between Strathblane and Killearn. Open: Monday to Saturday 10.00 - 16.00, Sundays 12.00 - 16.00 (Tours every hour).

THE MUSEUM OF AYRSHIRE COUNTRY LIFE AND COSTUME
Dalgarven Mill, Dalgarven,
Dalry Road, Kilwinning,
North Ayrshire, KA13 6PL
Tel: 01294 552448
Email: admin@dalgarvanmill.org

Thirty minutes from Prestwick Airport, this large group of stone mills, cottages and farm buildings now house a wonderful Museum of Rural Life and one of Scotland's finest Costume Collections. Restaurant with home baking, Antiques Shop, Riverside walks.

SHOPPING

When it comes to shopping, style-conscious Glasgow can hold its own with any big British city. Its new slogan – 'Scotland with Style' – says it all.

Princes Square, on Buchanan Street, is Scotland's leading specialty shopping centre, with five levels of retail outlets, bars and bistros in a stylish nineteenth-century building, which has been transformed into one of the city's favourite meeting places. The complex has the largest collection of up-market specialist shops under one roof anywhere in the UK. The wide selection of places to eat and drink means you could happily spend all day, or all weekend, browsing through what they have to offer. Outlets include the **Glasgow Room**, one of the city's most exciting commercial art galleries, and a huge assortment of designer names from **Calvin Klein** to **Monsoon**, **Reiss**, **Whistles** and **Ted Baker**.

Princes Square shopping centre

At junction 26 (eastbound) on Glasgow's M8 motorway, **Braehead** is the region's prime shopping and leisure mall. With a fantastic mix of retail outlets, bars and restaurants and leisure facilities, it's ideal for family shoppers. With more than one hundred top High Street stores, Braehead also has a curling rink, ice rink, riverside boardwalk, a 4000-seat sport and entertainment arena and a **Maritime Heritage Centre**.

High Quality
Silver & Gold Jewellery
of celtic, traditional & modern design

Manufacturing jewellers, based on the Island of South Uist in the Outer Hebrides since 1974.

Hebridean Jewellery

Carthouse Gallery and coffee shop at the Calgary Hotel on the Isle of Mull, Inner Hebrides

The west of Scotland has its own portfolio of Scottish brands purveying desirable products that are unique to the region. Among Scotland's finest craft products are handmade woollen knitwear, jewellery made to traditional designs from sterling silver and semi-precious stones and of course the world's finest whiskies. Galston, in Ayrshire, is the home of **Balmoral Knitwear,** who create quality woollen and cotton sports and leisure wear, as well as traditional Scottish applique and embroidery designs.

Look out too for the many outlets of the **Edinburgh Woollen Mill.** Much more than just a chain of stores offering quality Scottish knitwear at bargain prices, Edinburgh Woollen Mill's shops, offer a wide range of ladies and men's clothing, accessories and gift lines, along with luxury cashmere knits and traditional Scottish products including kilts, arans and clan tartans. The company also owns leisure sites and tourist attractions including **Designer Zones, Spirit of Scotland Whisky Shops, Ale Shops,** animal attractions and spinning and weaving exhibitions. Outlets across the west of Scotland are located in: Aberfoyle, Alexandria, Ayr, Clarkston, Coatbridge, Dumfries, Fort William, Glasgow, Gretna, Helensburgh, Inveraray, Kilmahog, Langholm, Moffat, New Lanark and Oban.

Continuing a long family tradition, the **Hebridean Jewellery** workshop at Iochdar, on remote South Uist in the Western Isles, produces superbly crafted silver and gold jewellery designed by its founder, John Hart, and his son, John M. Hart. At Lochdar and the Hebridean Jewellery shops in Fort William and in Stornoway on the island of Lewis, you'll find beautifully made kilt pins and thistle and Luckenbooth brooches. Heavy gold and silver wrist and neck torcs and penannular brooches that draw their inspiration from ancient Celtic and Pictish traditional designs are also available.

Finally, of course, there's the true, distilled essence of the west of Scotland: malt whisky. The perfect gift or long-lasting souvenir to bring back memories of your visit, fine single malts are sold everywhere. Probably the best place to buy your bottle of whisky, however, is right where it is made – at the distillery. The **Glengoyne Distillery** in Killearn on Loch

Ardbeg Single
Malt whisky,
Isle of Islay

Lomond, the **Bladnoch Distillery** near Wigtown in Galloway,
the **Oban Distillery** in Argyll, **Bowmore** on Jura and many
more across the western mainland and islands all offer the
chance to sip, savour and purchase the finest malts.

Loch Lomond Books and Internet Café is a brand new
bookstore based at Loch Lomond Shores, the
spectacular new shopping and leisure destination on
the banks of Loch Lomond, only 30 minutes from
Glasgow.

LISTINGS

BALMORAL MILL & COFFEE SHOP
Galston, Ayrshire, KA4 8HF
Tel: 00 44 1563 820213
Fax: 0044 1563 821740
Email: info@balmoralknitwear.co.uk
Web: www.balmoralmill.com
Open 7 Days (incl. Bank Holidays)

Balmoral Mill Shop sells cashmere &
lambswool, embroidered knitwear, bowling
& golf attire, Burnawn, Lyle & Scott,
Glenmuir, Farah, Gabicci, Alice Collins,
Tulchan and Tanya. For fantastic bargains,
call into our shop, only 25 minutes drive
from Prestwick Airport, or order on-line.

LOCH LOMOND BOOKS
AND INTERNET CAFÉ
Unit 5, The Retail Crescent,
Loch Lomond Shores,
Balloch, G83 8QP
Tel: +44 (0) 1389 750500
Email: info@lochlomondbooks.com

Loch Lomond Books and Internet Café is
a new bookstore housed in the
spectacular Lomond Shores at Balloch
30 minutes from Glasgow, stocking
books for all ages and interests.
Our café serves Italian coffee, pastries
and broadband access to the Internet.

Glasgow and the west of Scotland have an extensive portfolio of places to stay to suit all budgets, whether you are travelling on business, taking a family holiday or a short romantic break, or simply looking for an affordable place to lay your head after experiencing the city's rocking nightlife.

At the top end of the scale, the city centre's newest luxury hotel is the stylish **Radisson SAS**, which opened in 2002. Other international chain hotels in central Glasgow include the five-star **Hilton**, as well as **Jury's**, the **Marriott** and the **Moathouse**. Luxury accommodation in the city can be surprisingly affordable, with prices starting from as low as £70-£100 per room per night.

Glasgow also has its share of classy boutique hotels, and the **Devonshire Hotel** on Devonshire Gardens is one of Scotland's most romantic places to stay.

For alternative accommodation, there are lively inns such as **Rab Ha's**, on Hutcheson Street in the Merchant City district, a cheerful pub-restaurant and hotel, or **Babbity Bowster**, on Blackfriars Street, which is also a favourite live music venue.

There are plenty of guesthouses throughout the region, both in towns and smaller villages and in countryside locations. The

Central Hotel
Bothwell Street,
Glasgow

The impressive facade of the Marine Highland Hotel, South Ayrshire

Discover Scotland Network offers an information and booking service for some 280 self-catering holiday houses throughout Scotland.

During university vacations, the **University of Glasgow** offers affordable, comfortable accommodation in University halls of residence, including accommodation in en-suite, hotel-style rooms in the heart of the city. Visitors on an even tighter budget can opt for the newly refurbished **Glasgow Youth Hostel**. Alternatively, the **Scottish Youth Hostel Association** has a network of more than seventy hostels all over Scotland.

Ayrshire and the south west have plenty of quality accommodation to choose from, with a number of hotels and guesthouses within easy reach of Glasgow Prestwick Airport, the golf courses and other attractions. The **Golf View Hotel**, for example, is in an enviable position overlooking Prestwick Old Course, and is only minutes from the airport. Also in Prestwick, is the venerable three-star **Parkstone Hotel**, which has been owned and managed by the same family since it opened seventy-one years ago. Ideal for golfers, too, is

Strathtalus Country Guest House, a newly-built luxury villa with five en-suite rooms, next to the Brunston Castle golf clubhouse.

Ayr is a popular holiday base, with a good choice of friendly small hotels and guesthouses, such as the pretty, family-run **Daviot House,** just one minute from the sea. Right on the seafront, the privately owned, four-star **Fairfield House Hotel** combines Edwardian splendour and country house hospitality with a very modern style and a first class restaurant under the direction of award-winning head chef John Paul McLaughlan. Other friendly and comfortable places to stay include the **Kildonan,** at Queen's Terrace, and the **Kensington House.**

At Dunure, **Dunduff House** is set in a 650 acre estate which overlooks the Firth of Clyde. All the bedrooms have splendid views of Arran and the sea. Another good base for holidaymakers near Ayr is the **Finlayson Arms Hotel,** in the quiet country village of Coylton. This hotel has cosy rooms and a reputation for great homemade food.

Near Troon, Malcolm and Karen Simpson have opened the **Gailes Lodge Restaurant and Inn,** a 40-room hotel with spacious bedrooms and super-king size beds. Near Irvine, the **Annfield House Hotel** on the banks of the River Irvine, is the ideal location for a luxury romantic weekend break. Largs, on the Ayrshire coast, has plenty of couthy guesthouses, including the **Lea Mar Guesthouse,** with en-suite facilities and TVs in all the rooms, and the pleasant, four-star **Whin Park Guesthouse**.

On Arran, the **Breadalbane Hotel** in Kildonan, with breathtaking views of the islands of Ailsa Craig and Pladda, offers self-catering and hotel accommodation

The grounds of Culzean Castle-late 18th century mansion, South Ayrshire

on a sandy beach. The island's oldest inn, the **Lagg Inn** at Kilmory, has been offering a warm welcome for more than 200 years. In Brodick, the island's main village, the **Glenartney Hotel** is quiet, restful and ideal for families.

Down in Galloway, near Castle Douglas, **Craigadam** offers country house elegance within a working farm, with seven luxury, individually decorated and themed bedrooms and a cosy three-bedroom cottage for self-catering holidays.

Further a field, an excellent location for exploring the wilds of Skye, Argyll and the Western Isles is the **Kyle Hotel**, in Kyle of Lochalsh, which is only a stone's throw from Skye and easily accessible from Glasgow by road or rail.

ANNFIELD HOUSE HOTEL
6 Castle Street,
Irvine, KA12 8RJ
Tel: 0044 (0)1294 278903
Fax: 0044 (0)1294 278904
Email: Annfield@househotel.fsnet.co.uk
Web: www.Annfieldhousehotel.co.uk

1850 mansion house in centre of Irvine overlooking river. 9 miles (10 minutes) from Prestwick Airport Railway Station. 30 minutes from Glasgow. Close to all major Ayrshire Golf courses. Complementary bottle of wine for each Ryanair group staying and dining. Double from £35 per person.

BEST WESTERN KINLOCH HOTEL
Blackwaterfoot, Isle of Arran, KA27 8ET
Tel: 01770 860444
Fax: 01770 860447
Email: reservations@kinlochhotel.eclipse.co.uk
Web: www.kinloch-arran.com

Journey to Arran and the enjoy the Kinloch Hotel. Family owned & run for over 50 years. Open all year round the hotel offers 43 en-suite bedrooms and 7 luxury self-contained suites, indoor swimming pool and sauna, squash court & gym.

BREADLABANE HOTEL
Kildonan,
Isle of Arran,
KA27 8SE
Tel: 01770 820284
Email: yvonne@breadalbanehotel.co.uk

A warm and friendly coastal inn, beautifully furnished with stunning sea views overlooking the islands of Pladda and Ailsa Craig.
Relax and unwind with a malt whisky or real ale and an excellent home cooked meal.

CRAIGADAM COUNTRY HOUSE
Castle Douglas, DG7 3HU,
Dumfries and Galloway,
Scotland
Tel / Fax: 00441556 650233
Email: inquiry@craigadam.com
Web: www.craigadam.com

Craigadam is a large and elegant country house situated on an organic sheep farm with views southwards over rolling hills. The bedrooms are spacious and luxurious. The meals are presented with great attention to detail and the flavours are delightful.

DAVIOT HOUSE
12 Queens Terrace,
Ayr, KA7 1DU
Tel: 01292 269678
Fax: 01292 880567
Email: thedaviot@aol.com
Web: www.daviothouse.com

Daviot House Victorian guest house located minutes from town centre and one minute from seafront. All rooms ensuite starting at £24 per person. Ann a is member of South Ayrshire Advance Tee Booking service and happy to arrange your golf.
Tourist Board rated 3 Star. AA 4 Diamond.

DUNDUFF HOUSE
Dunure,
Ayr, Ayrshire, KA7 4LH
Tel: 01292 500225
Fax: 01292 500222
Email: gemmelldunduff@aol.com
Web: www.gemmelldunduff.co.uk

Dunduff is a Georgian country house set in a 650 acre estate dating as far back as the 15C. It stands proudly overlooking the firth of Clyde to Arran and the Mull of Kintyre of which all our bedrooms look onto. Many attractions nearby include Culzean Castle, Burns Heritage, golf and local walks.

FAIRFIELD HOUSE HOTEL
12 Fairfield Road,
Ayr, KA7 2AR
Tel: 01292 267461
Fax: 01292 261456
Email: reservations@fairfieldhotel.co.uk
Web: www.fairfieldhotel.co.uk

Located in centre of Ayr, 15 minutes from Prestwick Airport this former Victorian Mansion House set in a quiet residential area has 44 en-suite bedrooms, brasserie, fine dining restaurant, bar, lounge and leisure facilities. 4 Star RAC & AA.

FINLAYSON ARMS HOTEL
24 Hillhead,
Coylton,
Ayrshire, KA6 6JT,
Scotland
Tel: 00441292 570298
Fax: 00441292 571545

The Finlayson Arms is a friendly family run hotel, about 5 miles from the centre of Ayr. We have 8 bedrooms, all en-suite, a 42 – seater restaurant serving food all day, and a public bar. Private parking is at the rear of the hotel.

GLENARTNEY HOTEL
Mayish Road, Brodick,
Isle of Arran, KA27 8BX
Tel/Fax: 01770 302220
Mobile: 07771 846073
Email: info@glenartney-arran.co.uk
Web: www.glenartney-arran.co.uk

A relaxed no-smoking hotel, with breathtaking views, quietly situated close to the heart of Brodick. 10 ensuite bedrooms with colour TV. Excellent full Scottish breakfasts. Residents bar with a wide range of malts. Drying facilities and secure cycle/golf trolley storage.

GOLF VIEW
17/19 Links Road,
Prestwick, Ayrshire, KA9 1QG
Tel: +44 (0) 1292 671234 or 470396
Fax: +44 (0) 1292 671244
Email: welcome@golfviewhotel.com
Web: www.golfviewhotel.com

Located 2 kms. from Prestwick airport. 11 bedrooms, some overlooking the historic links of Prestwick GC. Also 3 self-catering chalets. Drinks licence. Smoking restricted. Tee times arranged. Easy access to Glasgow, Arran and all of Scotland and Northern England.

KENSINGTON HOUSE
37 Miller Road,
Ayr,
KA7 2AX
Tel: 01292 266301
Email: carolgrace49@aol.com

Close to the beach, we are 5 minutes walk from Ayr Town Centre. We have 3 en suite bedrooms including the Garden Suite with private conservatory. Twin, double & family rooms are available. We operate a strict no smoking policy.

KYLE HOTEL
40 – 42 Main Street,
Coylton,
Ayrshire, KA6 6JA
Tel: 0044 1292 570312
Fax: 0044 1292 571493
Open all year

A warm and friendly welcome awaits you at at the Kyle. Situated at the heart of Burns country only 10 mins from Ayr, Prestwick Airport only 15 mins. Ideal for Ayr Racecourse and many of Ayrshire's top golf courses.

LEA-MAR GUEST HOUSE
20 Douglas Street,
Largs, Ayrshire, KA30 8PS
Tel/Fax: 01475 672447
Email: leamar.guesthouse@fsbdial.co.uk
Web:
www.smoothhound.co.uk/hotels/leamar.html

Superb family run guesthouse. Four en-suite double/twin bedrooms. VisitScotland 3 Stars AA 4 Diamonds. North end of town, 25 miles from Glasgow and Prestwick Airports. Close to all amenities, good base to explore West Coast & Islands. From £27 per person.

STRATHTALUS COUNTRY GUEST HOUSE
4 Brunston Wynd, Dailly,
Nr Girvan, KA26 9GA
Tel: +44 (0) 1465 811425
Mob: +44 (0) 7971 550667
Email: rod@strathtalus.com
Web: www.strathtalus.com

4* Bed/Breakfast in rural Ayrshire, located on Brunston Castle Golf Course overlooking Carrick Hills and River Girvan. Open all year, offering 5 tastefully decorated en suite bedrooms with Sky TV, minifridges. 30 minutes drive from airport, debit/credit card payment facility, rates from £25.00 pp.

THE PARKSTONE HOTEL
Central Esplanade,
Prestwick, Ayrshire, KA9 1QN
Tel: 01292 477286
Fax: 01292 477671
Email: info@parkstonehotel.co.uk
Web: www.parkstonehotel.co.uk

Quality AA 3 Star Hotel located on Prestwick seafront, one mile from the airport, within walking distance of rail station, town centre and golf courses. The Hotel has an award winning AA Rosette restaurant, bar and 24 hour reception service.

THE KILDONAN
Queen's Terrace,
Ayr, KA7 1DX
Tel: 00441292 285122
Fax: 00441292 290105
Email: gillian@kildonan27.freeserve.co.uk
Web: www.thekildonanayr.co.uk

A Friendly welcome awaits you in our small family-run business. We are by the seafront yet only a few minutes walk from historic Ayr town centre and other amenities. Pretwick International Airport is a short drive away and Ayrshire is rich with magnificent golf courses and castles.

THE PARK HOTEL
Rugby Park, Kilmarnock,
KA1 2DP
Tel: 01563 545999
Fax: 01563 545322
Email: enquiries@theparkhotel.uk.com
Web: www.theparkhotel.uk.com

Set in the heart of Ayrshire our location allows you to enjoy the relaxing sites of Burns Country, with a host of premier golf courses within a 10-mile radius. The Park Hotel, Kilmarnock's only 4 star hotel is centrally located; with easy access to Prestwick and Glasgow airports.

WHIN PARK GUEST HOUSE
16 Douglas Street,
Largs, Ayrshire, KA30 8PS
Tel: +44(0)1475 673437
Fax: +44(0)1475 687291
Email: Ian@whinpark.co.uk
Web: www.whinpark.co.uk

Situated close to the seafront Whin Park is a 4 Star Guest House that provides an ideal base for touring. All rooms are en-suite, with TV & hospitality tray. 45 Minutes from Glasgow Prestwick Airport. Non Smoking. Parking available.

Glasgow has experienced a wining and dining revolution in the last decade and the range of places to eat has expanded enormously.

Perhaps the trendiest area in which to eat is the Merchant City district, where pubs and bistros such as **Babbity Bowster**, the **City Merchant** and **Café Gandolfi** helped to kick-start the transformation of Glasgow's dining experience. **Byres Road** and **Ashton Lane** are centres of dining excellence in the West End and are also richly endowed with good pubs and bars. In the city centre, between Sauchiehall Street and the river, you'll find Glasgow's largest concentration of international restaurants and big-chain dining outlets, while on the other side of the Clyde developments are taking place in the Southside district.

The variety of international cuisine from which to choose has widened too. Twenty years ago, exotic dining in Glasgow meant a trip to the row of Indian restaurants that stood along Renfield Street. Today, you can sample gourmet Indian cuisine with a modern twist at Nav Basi's new restaurant **Dhabba**, in the Merchant City district, or at Monir Mohammed's **Mother India**. Sushi bars, Chinese and Thai restaurants abound, Spanish-style tapas bars are plentiful, and there's first-rate Greek cuisine on offer at places like **Antonious** at Charing Cross.

Glasgow and Italy have been closely linked for more than a century, and the Scots-Italian community has spawned scores of Italian restaurants, such as the casually modern **Wellington Street Café** in central Glasgow or the superb **La Parmigiana**, which offers the best of Italian cooking.

Glasgow has also moved with the times for vegetarians. A decade ago, those looking for a meat-free meal might have had to settle for a salad, a cheese sandwich or an omelette, but the city now has an assortment of meat-free eating places. Many mainstream restaurants also offer vegetarian menu options.

At the top end of the range, Glasgow has more than a dozen excellent restaurants which can hold their own against Britain's best. Old favourites, including **Rogano**, the **Buttery**, and the long-established **Ubiquitous Chip**, must now compete with the likes of **Chardon d'Or, Gamba, Rococo, Stravaigin', Lux, Smiths of Glasgow, Quigleys, Saint Judes, Air Organic, Battlefield Rest**, and **Otago**.

Lower down the budget scale, the best bet is to head for one of the bars and gastro-pubs that have sprung up all over Glasgow and western Scotland. The region's

favourite pub meal, pie, beans and chips – is still cheap, filling and omnipresent (if not overly healthy). Alongside such offerings, you can expect to find pubs serving freshly prepared meals using ingredients from Scottish farms, seas and rivers.

The Scottish restaurant renaissance has been based on new and more imaginative ways of using some of the world's best produce – venison from the deer forests of Perthshire, lamb from the Border hills, Aberdeen Angus beef and freshly-caught seafood from the Atlantic. Moreover, because of Scotland's small size, wherever it comes from, be it hand-dived scallops or wild salmon caught in an Argyll sea loch, it is guaranteed to be fresh.

Nor is fine dining restricted to the big city. There are great places to eat all over western Scotland. Seafood is especially good, with outfits such as the legendary **Loch Fyne Seafood and Smokery** at Loch Fyne in Argyll, which has become a place of pilgrimage for connoisseurs of oysters, kippers and smoked salmon in all its guises.

Also on the shores of Loch Fyne at Strathlachlan, is **Inver Cottage**, a pleasant bistro offering real home-cooking in pleasant surroundings. Near Waternish on Skye, **Lochbay Seafood** is equally popular, and in Oban the **Waterfront Restaurant**, next to the station, has the best grub in town.

South of the Clyde, **Fouters** in Ayr has been established for more than twenty-five years and is something of a local legend, serving only the finest local produce. For the heartiest pub grub in the region – very welcome after a bracing round of golf – try the steak pie at the **Wheatsheaf** at Symington, between Ayr and Prestwick. Seafood fans will like **Fins**, in Fairlie (close to Largs), which has its own fish farm and smokery.

Glasgow is a city that likes to go out and after-dark entertainment ranges from ballet, opera and theatre to down-and-dirty garage, country and rock music. To find out what's on during your visit, pick up a copy of 'The List', central Scotland's comprehensive listings magazine, which profiles the full gamut of entertainment, from popular to high culture.

For a complete night out, from pre-dinner drinks and dinner followed by late-night clubbing, all under one roof, seek out hybrid, stylish venues which combine bars, dance clubs and restaurants, like the **Corinthian** on Ingram Street.

For a full-on pub crawl without ever stepping out onto the street, the legendary and labyrinthine **Waxy O'Connor's Glasgow**, on West George Street has six unique bars – each with its own atmosphere – on three levels, all connected by a maze of stairs and passages. Located

Cresswell Street in Glasgow's West End

next to Queen Street station, it is close to all the main shopping and commercial areas, admission is free and the dress code is smart/casual.

Frankenstein Glasgow, also on West George Street, is another spot offering all-day and late night entertainment, with an extensive breakfast, lunch and dinner menu. Experience, not only a great party atmosphere, but thrills and chills as the Monster comes to life and roams the building.

Glasgow has fostered some of Britain's biggest bands, including Texas, Travis and Oasis, who were discovered by a local entrepreneur whilst playing in **King Tut's Wah Wah Hut** – the cheerful floating venue on the Clyde. Other well known Glaswegian names in the music world include: Simple Minds, Wet Wet Wet, Del Amitri, Primal Scream, the Cosmic Rough Riders and Belle & Sebastian.

Musicians strike up with an impromptu session in a bar during the Celtic Connections Music Festival, Glasgow

The city is well supplied with venues from the historic **Barrowland ballroom** in the East End to the brick-vaulted **Arches**, beneath Central Station, which throbs with club events year round.

Other top clubbing sites include the internationally acclaimed **Sub Club**, hosting Subculture. **Tiger Tiger**, **The Tunnel** and **Arta** attract an older, more laid-back and style conscious audience, while the **Garage** offers cheap drinks and attracts the student crowd. Other student venues include **Divine** at the Art School student union, **Barfly**, beside the river, and the **Riverside Club**, which offers ceilidh entertainment until midnight, then turns, Cinderella-style, into a club. On a tight budget, head for **Ad Lib** or **Lowdown**, cool bars, which play club sounds but don't charge door fees.

Around town, a full portfolio of pubs and bars such as **Nice 'n' Sleazy** and the **13th Note** provide venues for up-and-coming local talent. **Glasgow's Centre for Contemporary Arts** offers a challenging programme of new music, while the **Renfrew Ferry** has become the city's top spot for roots and world music. The **Carling Academy**, which opened in the Southside in 2003, has also become one of the city's favoured rock venues.

Glasgow's newest arts and entertainment venue is **OranMor**, which opened this year at the top of Byers Road, in the heart of the West End. The former Kelvinside parish church has been renovated and converted into a state of the art drama and music venue at a cost of more than £6 million. It now hosts original theatre from leading Scottish playwrights such as William McIlvanney, Anna Burnside and Dave Anderson.

Until the end of 2004, OranMor is presenting a season of contemporary Scottish plays at lunchtime, under the banner 'A Play, a Pie and a Pint' - which says it all, really. OranMor lifted the idea from Dublin, where a similar theatre season of lunchtime pub drama proved a big hit. Several Irish playwrights are bringing their work to OranMor as part of the season.

OranMor play host to regular gigs by leading Scottish bands, including a recent curtain-raiser for the venue by Capercaillie, Scotland's longest established traditional-rock crossover ensemble.

For those whose tastes run to classical music, ballet and dance, Glasgow has plenty to offer. The **Clyde Auditorium**, next to the Scottish Exhibition and Conference Centre – locally known as **'the Armadillo'** because of its advanced design – hosts leading classical ensembles from all over the world, in addition to rock and pop performers. The **Royal Concert Hall** and the **Theatre Royal**, home to both Scottish Opera and the adventurous Scottish Ballet with its broadly based repertoire of contemporary dance, are also renowned. Thanks to the National Lottery, the

consistently challenging **Citizens' Theatre**, in the Gorbals district, has recently been renovated and is one of Britain's best. The **Tron Theatre** at Trongate offers modern Scottish theatre, whilst the **Glasgow Film Theatre** in Rose Street is the city's premier arthouse cinema.

Throughout western Scotland, there's plenty more entertainment and nightlife to choose from. In smaller towns, nightlife still tends to be pub-based, but you'll find plenty to enjoy, especially at weekends – from home-grown Scottish rock to traditional ceilidh entertainment with fiddle music, Gaelic singing and Scottish country dancing. The southwest is especially lively between August and October, when venues across the region host **Gael Force**, a celebration of Scottish and Celtic culture that offers a tempest of arts and entertainment across Dumfries and Galloway. With classical music, poetry, jazz, art workshops, stand-up comedy, film and the visual arts and traditional music and dancing, it is sure to be a jubilant event.

A bar situated in the town of Stirling

EDINBURGH

Edinburgh's heritage and history has attracted visitors in droves since Sir Walter Scott put the city on the tourist map in the nineteenth century. Of late the city has gained a reputation of being a hub of entertainment and is home to some of Europe's top nightlife venues.

This is partly down to Scotland's liberal licensing laws, which allow pubs and music venues to stay open almost around the clock. It could also have something to do Edinburgh's annual **Hogmanay** celebrations, which have become world-famous and draw thousands of tourists who bring in the New Year with top-level bands and entertainers. They are also witnesses to the dazzling firework display at the stroke of midnight.

Ross Fountain in Princes Street Gardens West

Fireworks over Edinburgh Castle and the Balmoral Clock at the end of the Edinburgh International Festival

The famous **Edinburgh International Festival** has played a key role in developing cultural tourism in the region and runs for almost two months during the summer. Ironically though, it's the **Festival Fringe** – originally an informal calendar of events by amateurs, student drama groups and up-and-coming bands and comedy performers – which has become the more popular event. It has gained itself a higher profile among younger visitors than the Edinburgh Festival.

The Royal Mile, crowded with visitors and performers during the Fringe festival

But behind all that lies what made Edinburgh a great place to visit in the first place – a rich heritage, a clutch of superbly evocative historic attractions, and its superb setting. To the south of the city are the **Pentland Hills**. The **Firth of Forth** and the **Fife Hills** lie to the north and in the centre of the city is Edinburgh's own pet mountain, **Arthur's Seat**.

Edinburgh's history begins in the seventh century AD, when King Edwin of Northumbria built a fort atop **Castle Rock**, the 328 ft crag, which dominates the city centre and can be seen from all over Edinburgh. Over the next 1,000 years the castle grew into one of Britain's mightiest fortresses, and is still impressive today. Kilted sentries guard its mighty gates and there are fantastic views from the ramparts and from the Castle Esplanade, outside the castle gates. Within are the imposing **Royal Apartments** and the **Crown Room**, which houses the **regalia of Scotland** and the legendary **Stone of Destiny**.

Edinburgh's Old Town, with its multi-storey medieval tenements, spreads downhill to either side of the Royal Mile, which connects the Castle with **Holyrood Palace** and the still-unfinished **Scottish Parliament** building. Worth visiting if you're walking down the famous Mile are the **Scotch Whisky Heritage Centre,** just outside the Castle, the **High Kirk,** founded in 1120 and the **Lady Stair's House** – now the **Writers' Museum,** which is packed with memorabilia and manuscripts by Burns, Scott and R.L. Stevenson.

The **Museum of Childhood** is full of toys and games from all over the world. It's a great day out for families and children of all ages. If it doesn't manage to captivate you perhaps the more modern attractions of **Dynamic Earth** will, where interactive video displays highlight the secrets of the Earth's geology.

Outdoor terrace of Oloroso, Edinburgh

South of the Castle and the Royal Mile lie the old **Grassmarket district**, the **University of Edinburgh** and two excellent museums, the new **Museum of Scotland**, which opened in 1998, and the **Royal Museum**. Connected by a walkway, they highlight Scotland's history and culture from the earliest times to the present day. They're the perfect choice on rainy days or for dining in, as there is an excellent restaurant as well. North of the centre, crowned by picturesque nineteenth century follies and monuments, is **Calton Hill** and the gracious crescents of the **New Town,** dating back to the eighteenth century.

Royal Yacht Britannia

One of the top visitor attractions of this area lies at the foot of **Leith Walk**, a former dockland area, which has become one of the city's prime residential and retail districts and home to the former **Royal Yacht Britannia**, now moored beside the glittering new **Ocean Terminal**.

LISTINGS

CELTIC TRAILS
17 Falcon Gardens, Edinburgh, EH10 4AP
Tel: 0044131 4775416/9
Fax: 0044131 4775419
Mobile: 00447879 838401
Email: jac@celtictrails.co.uk
Web: www.celtictrails.co.uk

Well established and truly unique half/full day excursions in small groups to historic and sacred sites near Edinburgh, including Rosslyn Chapel. Complimentary notes, maps and refreshments. Personalised tours cover myths and legends of Celtic saints, Arthur & Merlin, and Knights Templar.

EDINBURGH BUTTERFLY & INSECT WORLD
Dobbies Garden World, Melville Nursery, Lasswade, Midlothian, EH18 1AZ
Tel: 0131 663 4932 Fax: 0131 654 2774
Email:
info@Edinburgh-butterfly-world.co.uk
Web: www.edinburgh-butterfly.world.co.uk

Its Creeping, Its Crawling. It's a JUNGLE in there! Indoor tropical rainforest with thousands of beautiful exotic butterflies and plants. The bugs and beasties exhibition features hundreds of creepy crawlies, reptiles and frogs. Daily "Meet the Beasties" handling sessions!

View from Calton Hill

THE LOTHIANS

South of Edinburgh and the Forth lie the Lothians, a region of farming villages and former coalmining towns, studded with historic castles and some of Scotland's finest golf courses.

The **Pentland Hills** are ideal for picturesque summer walks and skiing in winter, while the **Firth of Forth** offers boat trips to its archipelago of rocky islets, uninhabited, except for seals and seabirds.

West of the capital, the famed **Forth Bridges** are feats of engineering connecting Edinburgh with Fife; and close to the shores of the Firth is one of Scotland's most imposing stately homes – **Hopetoun House**.

Nearby, **Rosslyn Chapel** is a remarkable fifteenth century church, renowned for its elaborate sculptures and is said to have connections with the occult Templar order. Featuring in the recent bestseller, *The Da Vinci Code*, the chapel has become a place of pilgrimage for those who believe its sculptures contain the key to ancient

secrets. Still further west at **Linlithgow** is the shell of the royal palace and birthplace of Mary, Queen of Scots. Destroyed in 1746, what remains of the castle overlooks Linlithgow Loch.

There are other impressive castle ruins east of the city, on the North Sea coast, at **Dunbar** and **Tantallon** and at the massive clifftop fortress of the **Red Douglases**. In summer there are boat trips from North Berwick to the Bass Rock, which is home to vast colonies of seabirds and the **Scottish Seabird Centre**, where you can learn more about the birdlife of the Firth.

Along the Forth coast, between Edinburgh and Berwick, there are windswept beaches and two of Scotland's top golf courses, at **Musselburgh**, which claims to rival St Andrews as the birthplace of golf, and **Gullane**. Other attractions include **Edinburgh Butterfly and Insect World**, five miles south of Edinburgh towards Dalkeith on the A7 highway. Colourful butterflies of every breed fly in its tropical forest alongside other exotic insects and creepie-crawlies.

It's easy to explore the Lothians by yourself, by bus, train or with a rented car but you can learn more by joining an escorted tour to the region's main attractions. **Celtic Trails Tour Company** offers a unique series of personalised half-day and whole-day tours from Edinburgh to the region's castles, country gardens and mythical sites of prehistoric, Celtic and medieval interest.

The grounds of Mellerstain House - an 18th century mansion

THE BORDERS

The rolling hills of the Border country, between the Lothians and the River Tweed, are steeped in history and dotted with ruined medieval abbeys and castle keeps.

This is a region of open moors, sheep pastures and pleasant market towns and it is also the heartland of Scottish rugby. Those with an interest in Scotland's history will find plenty to see here, from the dramatic ruins of Jedburgh and Melrose Abbeys to its numerous ruined castles. **Floors Castle**, near Kelso, home to the Roxburghe family is furnished with antiques and is surrounded by landscaped gardens. **Mellerstain**, also near Kelso, was built by the Adam brothers, the architects of Edinburgh's New Town, in 1725, and is one of Scotland's most outstanding Georgian stately homes. **Ferniehurst Castle**, near Jedburgh, is still in the possession of the Marquess of Lothian, chief of the Kerr family.

Melrose, with its great twelfth century abbey, is one of the region's prettiest towns. Among its many attractions is **Trimontium**, opposite the abbey, which is an interesting exhibition that focuses on finds from the ancient Roman fortress, unearthed at Eildon, in the hills above the town. **Dryburgh Abbey**, near Melrose, has suffered the ravages of time moreso than its neighbour but also merits a visit. **Abbotsford House**, built in 1822 was the home of the great nineteenth century romantic novelist Sir Walter Scott. Scott had a passion for mementoes from his country's history and the house has an armoury of relics: Bonnie Dundee's flintlock pistol and Rob Roy MacGregor's claymore.

There are more relics of Scotland's past at **Traquair House**, which was built in the twelfth century and is said to be the oldest continually inhabited house in Scotland. Its Jacobite owners locked Traquair's gates after Charles Edward Stuart's defeat in 1745, vowing not to open them until a Stuart monarch returned to the throne. The gates are still locked, but the house's collection of Jacobite relics is open to the public. **Thirlestane House**, near Lauder, the family home of the Duke of Lauderdale has incredibly grand interiors, though the servants' quarters, kitchens and nurseries are on a more human scale.

Traquair House - the oldest continually inhabited house in Scotland

FIFE

Nicknamed the 'beggar's mantle fringed with gold' because of its sandy beaches, the **Kingdom of Fife**, as it is still proudly known, lies between the Firth of Forth in the south and the Firth of Tay in the north. Conveniently close to Edinburgh by road and rail, the towns and villages of southern Fife have become part of the capital's commuter belt.

Firth of Forth towards the Forth rail bridge-built between 1883-90

Dunfermline, only 20 minutes from Edinburgh by train, was once the capital of Scotland, and the remains of its medieval grandeur include the ruins of an eleventh-century **Benedictine abbey**. It was also the birthplace of the millionaire philanthropist, **Alexander Carnegie**, and the weaver's cottage where he was born is now the **Alexander Carnegie Birthplace Museum**.

On the shores of Loch Leven, midway between Dunfermline and Perth, is **Kinross** and its grim island castle where Mary, Queen of Scots was imprisoned. Another royal relic is **Falkland Palace**; an exemplar of Renaissance architecture built in 1541 and used as a hunting lodge and country seat by Stuart monarchs.

At the small village of **Ceres,** a different facet of Scottish life is revealed by the **Fife Folk Museum**, which focuses on the daily life of ordinary villagers and farmers.

The **Fife Coastal Path** passes through a string of small fishing villages, including: **Pittenweem** and the nearby

Kellie Castle; **Anstruther** and its **Scottish Fisheries Museum**; and **Crail**, prettiest of the Fife coast villages, with its thirteenth-century church, sixteenth-century Tollbooth, and a fishing harbour surrounded by traditional houses.

But Fife's biggest tourist draw is almost certainly **St Andrews**, which is home to the **Royal and Ancient Golf Club** and Scotland's oldest university, attended by **HRH Prince William**. St Andrews is a picturesque town in a great location with sweeping views of the North Sea coast and long sandy beaches. The ruins of its medieval castle and bottle dungeon and the remains of **St Andrews Cathedral** are both dramatic and spooky.

A more recent family attraction is the **Sea Life Centre**, which has touch pools where kids can get close to skates, rays and other creatures of the deep. The centre also has an outdoor seal pool. You can see wild seals in large numbers at low tide off the beaches of **Tentsmuir Nature Reserve**; a huge expanse of dunes between St Andrews and the mouth of the **River Tay**.

The town of St. Andrews, looking north from St. Rules tower, Fife

Another recently opened manmade attraction nearby is **Scotland's Secret Bunker**, a relic of the **Cold War** which was intended to shelter selected politicians, civil servants and military commanders in case of nuclear attack.

Arbroath, an industrial town and resort, North East of Dundee

ANGUS

North of the silvery Tay, **Angus** is the farming and fishing hinterland of **Dundee**, Scotland's lively, fourth largest city. It combines city life with rural attractions such as the **Angus glens** – Glen Prosen, Glen Clova and Glen Isla – and the foothills of the **Grampian Highlands**. The Tay forms a broad firth almost three miles across where it meets the sea east of Dundee, and road and rail bridges connect the city with Fife to the south.

Dundee was once noted for 'jute, jam and journalism' and, though DC Thompson's newspaper and comic empire survives to this day (publishing the **Beano** and other well loved comics), the jute and jam industries have vanished.

Dundee has reinvented itself as a centre of excellence for biotechnology, medicine and new technology and, with two universities and a prominent art college, it has earned a reputation for youthful nightlife and great pubs.

Top attractions here include the polar research vessel *Discovery*, built in a Dundee shipyard for Captain R.F. Scott's voyages to the Antarctic. Now, with its

The *RRS Discovery*, the ship that Captain Scott sailed to Antarctica that was originally built in Dundee

adventuring days over, it is moored on the waterfront at **Discovery Point**, along with the wooden frigate *Unicorn*, built in 1846.

Verdant Works, a state of the art visitor attraction within the last of Dundee's weaving mills, is well worth a visit and the new **Dundee Contemporary Arts Centre** has earned a nationwide reputation for exhibitions by cutting-edge artists.

Inland from Dundee, near Forfar, **Glamis Castle**, the birthplace of the late **Queen Mother**, is one of Scotland's grand aristocratic places. The **Angus Folk Museum** can be found nearby.

On the Angus coast, **Carnoustie** is one of Scotland's golfing hubs, regularly hosting Open events. **Monifieth**

Barry Mill, a working 18th century mill, West of Carnoustie

also has good golf courses, while the fishing town of **Arbroath** is famed for its smoked haddock ('smokies') and its ruined **Abbey**, where the **Declaration of Arbroath** was signed, affirming Scotland's independence from England in the fourteenth century.

The Atholl
Gathering and
Highland Games

PERTHSHIRE

Perthshire, the largest Scottish county, is truly the gateway to the Highlands. This county combines wild, empty hills and glens, heathery grouse moors and deer forests with gentler farming country to the south, along the banks of the River Tay, which flows through Perthshire from its source in **Loch Tay** and opens into a broad tidal estuary, the Firth of Tay, at Perth.

The main highway to **Inverness** and the northwest, the A9, follows the Tay for much of the way north, passing through increasingly striking scenery. Both the Tay and Perthshire's other major river, the **Earn**, offer some of the best (and most expensive) trout and salmon fishing in the world. This excellent fishing, along with deerstalking and grouse and pheasant shooting, makes Perthshire Scotland's poshest county, attracting droves of England's elite from south of the Border during the hunting, shooting and fishing seasons.

Perth is more of a market town and shopping centre than a tourist trap, but its attractions include the **Fergusson Gallery**, dedicated to the works of the painter J.D. Fergusson, and the regimental museum of the **Black Watch**, housed in the regiment's headquarters in **Balhousie Castle**, on Hay Street. Perth also boasts a handsome fifteenth-century church, **St John's Kirk**, on John Street.

Scone, the earliest capital of the Scots kings, is only two miles from Perth. **Scone Palace**, built in 1803, contains magnificent tapestries, antique furniture, glassware and eighteenth-century porcelain.

Dunkeld, prettily located on the upper Tay, is notable for its fifteenth-century cathedral and a graceful nineteenth-century bridge spanning the river. Also on the Tay, **Pitlochry** is a popular tourist stopover.

Just seven miles north is **Blair Castle**, looking just as a Highland potentate's stronghold should look, with whitewashed walls, turrets and arrow-slit windows. Blair is the home of the Duke of Atholl, the only man in Britain allowed to keep a private army, and inside the walls of the castle are displays of Highland arms and armour.

The Moulin Inn, Moulin, Pitlochry, Perthshire

Aberfeldy, near Loch Tay, is a popular holiday base for anglers and water sports enthusiasts. **Castle Menzies**, just outside the town, houses a small museum dedicated to the Menzies clan. Aberfeldy also has **Dewar's World of Whisky**, a slick introductory tour to whisky-making in the former **Aberfeldy Distillery**.

West of Perth, the small town of **Crieff** is home to a rival attraction, the **Famous Grouse Experience**, dedicated to promoting its own well-known label in the picturesque old **Glenturret distillery**.

Edinburgh has world-class shopping, from the Royal Mile stores, which sell Scottish tartans, woollen and cashmere knitwear, silver jewellery and tourist souvenirs, to elegant designer boutiques and big name stores. On the Royal Mile, **Geoffrey** (at 57-59 High Street) is the place for male visitors to kit themselves out in full Highland regalia of kilt, sporran and accessories.

Regardless of your provenance, there's a tartan to suit all tastes along the Royal Mile. For made-to-measure hand-sewn kilts and jackets and for all your highland accessories, **Clan Albanach**'s experienced staff will help find the kilt for you. While if you fancy a sporran that's a little out of the ordinary, they come in fluffy pink, lemon yellow, or electric blue these days.

The window of a kilt shop on the Royal Mile, Edinburgh

George Street, on the southern edge of the New Town, is where you'll find designer names such as **Coast** and **Karen Millen**. The recent arrival of a **Harvey Nichols** store on St Andrew Square, at the east end of George Street, has confirmed the capital's status as a shopper's paradise.

Princes Street is lined with the usual High Street names, but its flagship store, **Jenner's**, is an Edinburgh institution that has been trading from the same premises for more than a century and claims to be the world's oldest department store. **Princes Mall**, next to Waverly Station, has an array of chainstore clothing, accessory and souvenir outlets, cut-price bookstores, expresso bars and an excellent food hall, making it ideal for shopping and browsing in. At the top of Leith Walk, near the east end of Princes Street, the **St James Centre** is another run of the mill mall and is connected to the adjoining **John Lewis** store by a walkway.

Cockburn Street, running from the Royal Mile down towards Waverley Station, is where Edinburgh's students have shopped for cutting-edge fashion for the

Jenner's
Department Store,
Princes Street,
Edinburgh.

last thirty years. Lined with 'new age' jewellery and accessory stores, the shops here favour distressed denim and leather, Goth black, and clubbing wear. Those who were at college in the 1960s may be surprised to find their original flares and velvets on sale in shops like **Pie in the Sky**.

As a university town, Edinburgh has a varied selection of bookshops. **James Thin's** on Nicholson Street has been supplying books to the student populace since the mid-eighteenth century. **Forbidden Planet**, on Southbridge, provides close encounters of the science fiction, fantasy and graphic novel kind, whereas the more commercialised **Waterstone's** on George Street stocks the latest bestselling fact and fiction.

Scotland's capital is also a world centre for antiquarian books, art and antiques, with numerous private galleries selling the works of contemporary Scottish artists. **St Stephen Street**, in the trendy, bohemian Stockbridge district north of the New Town, is the place to hunt for tat and genuine antique finds too. It's home to several commercial art galleries as well.

Outside the capital, Dundee, St Andrews and Perth have the usual array of High Street stores such as **Marks and Spencers**, **Boots** and **Woolworths**. The **Edinburgh Woollen Mill** chain, sell the best of Scottish woollen and cashmere knitwear and accessories, has outlets throughout the city. Their stores stretch across the east of Scotland to Blairgowrie, Crieff, Cupar, Dundee, Jedburgh, Melrose, Peebles, Perth and St Andrews.

Country towns such as Dunkeld and Crieff often have antique bargains to offer in smaller, more personal stores and antique centres. Collectors can hunt out authentic Scottish antiques such as Mauchline ware and silverware at local antique centres such as the **Becca Gauldie Antiques Centre**, at Glendoick, midway between Perth and Dundee. For those in search of tartan kitsch, **Pitlochry**, on the road to the Highlands, has probably the biggest collection of Scottish souvenirs and paraphernalia of any Scottish town.

On Dundee's waterfront, **City Quay** is a new retail development, which offers a blend of shopping and family leisure only a few minutes walk from the city centre.

The Piob Mhor Tartan Shop at Blairgowrie a small town on the River Ericht, Perth & Kinross

In the very heart of Dundee the dazzling **Overgate Centre** – a futuristic, glass-fronted mall – has more than seventy top name stores. These include Scotland's second largest **Debenhams** outlet, the largest **H&M** store in Scotland, **Gap**, **GapKids** and many more, along with cafés and parking space for more than one thousand cars.

The innovative **Dundee Farmers Market** takes place on **Reform Street** on the third Saturday of the month (from January to October) and provides outlets for local producers selling everything from free-range ostrich steaks to Angus beef and organically grown fruit and vegetables.

Perth's pedestrianised **High Street** offers a wide range of speciality stores and major brand names. **Perth** is a happy hunting ground for Scottish antiques and as the gateway to the Tay's angling waters, Perth is also well supplied with fishing tackle suppliers and with camping and outdoor specialists. Just north of Perth, at **Bankfoot**, the **Scottish Liqueur Centre** sells hand-made chocolates and locally distilled liqueurs, works of art and gifts.

Edinburgh is well supplied with accommodation to suit all budgets. Major international hotel chains represented in the city include **Hilton National, Intercontinental** and **Sheraton**. Home-grown luxury is supplied by the **New Balmoral Hotel** (next to Waverley Station) and the **Caledonian Hotel** (at the west end of Princes Street), both are grand and sumptuous relics of the great railway-age of the nineteenth century.

A newer arrival on the luxury scene is the **Scotsman Hotel,** just off the Royal Mile on North Bridge, located in the former headquarters of the Scotsman newspaper. Also convenient to the city centre and Edinburgh's theatre district are the **Point Hotel**, on Bread Street, a style conscious property in a converted supermarket, and the **Apex International** and **Apex City hotels**, both on the Grassmarket. **Swallow hotels** have three star accommodation, at reasonable rates, in Edinburgh and Glasgow and quaint country houses in more secluded locations throughout Scotland and the UK.

Boutique-style properties include **Channings**, on South Learmouth Gardens, where a row of Edwardian townhouses have been turned into a stylish, 48-room hotel, and **Malmaison**, on the Shore in newly trendy

The elegant elliptical curves of Coates Crescent and Atholl Crescent, Edinburgh

Enjoy a stay with us
from only £25 pppn

Swallow Dundee

Swallow Hotels is one of the UKs most popular hotels chains and now has 28 three star hotels throughout the UK. London & Edinburgh Inns offer a diverse range of 31 individually styled hotels ranging from luxury country houses to country inns with character.

Combined, we can offer a choice of 59 locations to suit your needs. With 2 hotels within easy reach of Glasow/Prestwick Airport; 5 hotels 20 minutes from Aberdeen Airport and The Swallow Churchgate Hotel at Old Harlow is just 12 miles from Stansted Airport. For more details on locations and prices simply call the number below or visit www.swallowhotels.com or www.londonandedinburghinns.com

SWALLOW
HOTELS

LONDON & EDINBURGH
INNS

To book or for more information about Swallow Hotels call:
0870 600 4 666
quote ref RSWI

To book or for more information about London & Edinburgh Inns call:
0870 242 2841
quote ref RLEI

All prices include breakfast and are based on two people sharing a twin or double room for two consecutive nights. The offer is based on midweek tariff prices. Offer is subject to availability until 31st December 2004. Offer not valid in conjunction with any offer and applies to new bookings only. PPPN = Per Person Per Night.

Leith. The **Roxburghe,** on Charlotte Square, exudes a whiff of New Town style, with fireplaces designed by Robert Adam and rooms furnished with period antiques.

On the budget front, the **Scottish Youth Hostel Association** has five comfortable and central hostels. The SYHA also has dozens of hostels at strategic locations throughout the Borders, Angus, Fife and Perthshire.

The newest privately-run hostel in the capital is **Caledonian Backpackers** on Queensferry Street, which has dorm beds, single and double rooms and a huge, late-opening bar. **Edinburgh Backpackers**, on Cockburn Street, **Princes Street East Backpackers**, on West Register Street, and **Castle Rock Hostel**, on Johnston Terrace, also come recommended.

Though there is a higher concentration of guesthouses south of the city centre, they can be found all over the city. If you plan to visit during the Edinburgh International Festival or over Hogmanay, booking ahead is essential.

The tourist information office at 3 Princes Street (next to Waverley Station and above the Princes Mall shopping centre) can help you find accommodation all year round and **Edinburgh & Lothians Tourist Board** (www.edinburgh.org) operates a year-round online booking service.

Outside Edinburgh, there is a wide selection of places to stay, with plenty of friendly, family-run guesthouses and B&Bs. Many smaller properties do, however, close over the winter.

Booking ahead is always advisable in high season (July and August). You can book rooms on **Visit Scotland's web site:** www.visitscotland.com or by calling: 0845-225 5121.

St. Andrews Bay Hotel, Fife

There are fewer luxury hotels to be found outside Edinburgh, but among the exceptions there are some famous names, many of them associated with world-renowned golf courses. **Gleneagles**, built in the 1920s and still one of the world's finest hotels, with three championship golf courses, riding, shooting, fishing and a luxurious health club and spa.

In St Andrews, the **Old Course Hotel, Golf Resort and Spa** offers five-star suites and spa facilities, as well as superb access to the town's famed golf courses. Rivalling it is the **St Andrews Bay Golf Resort and Spa**, with 209 five-star rooms and a new **Clubhouse restaurant** overlooking the eighteenth holes of the Torrance and Devlin courses. At Carnoustie, north of Dundee, the **Carnoustie Golf Course Hotel** offers four-star comfort next to the **Carnoustie Championship course**.

In the Lothians and Borders, the **Roxburghe Hotel** near Kelso is owned and run by the local nobility, the **Duke and Duchess of Roxburghe**, and has real country-house flair and an 18-hole golf course.

On the North Sea coast, the **Marine Hotel** at North Berwick is an old seaside hotel of similar vintage to Gleneagles but has recently had a £10 million refit by its owners, **Macdonald Hotels**, with the addition of major-league leisure facilities. For something cosier, try the nearby **Open Arms**, at Dirleton, overlooked by a ruined castle in the centre of a pretty village.

Like the rest of Scotland, Edinburgh has experienced a restaurant revolution and caters for the tightest of budgets to the most refined gourmet palate. In the city centre, there's a restaurant, gastro pub, café-brasserie or vegetarian bistro every few yards.

Edinburgh has always had plenty of fine pubs that serve up the best of pub grub. There are venerable venues such as **Sandy Bell's** on Forrest Hill, a magnet for folk musicians, or **Bennet's**, in Tollcross, with its legendary array of whiskies. **Greyfriars Bobby**, on Candlemaker Row, is a kitsch landmark – opposite it is the statue of the loyal wee dog that inspired the pub's name. **Clark's Bar**, on Dundas Street, is a classic old Edinburgh boozer with old-fashioned red leather benches and mirrors. On Young Street, the **Oxford Bar** is another time-warped classic that has been made legendary by the Edinburgh crime writer Ian Rankin.

The **Café Royal**, with its long bar, elegant interior and attached oyster bar, is a must, and the **Doric**, on Market Street next to Waverley Station, is another great place to eat. Newer café-bars and bistros rival these old favourites. The **City Café** on Blair Street, just off the Royal Mile, was one of the first and is still among the best of Edinburgh's dining establishments. **North Bridge**, the brasserie-bar of the Scotsman Hotel on North Bridge, is also highly rated, as are the original **Howie's** on Bruntsfield Place and its spin-offs, **Howie's Stockbridge** at Glanville Place and **Howie's Waterloo** on Waterloo Place. **Skipper's**, on Dock Place in Leith, pioneered good food in the poshed-up docklands and is still going strong. Also in Leith, **The Shore** (on the Shore) is another favourite for exquisite seafood. The **Malmaison Brasserie**, on Tower Place, is a great location to eat on one of Edinburgh's rare sunny days.

Dome Bar and Restaurant, George Street, Edinburgh

For home fare, the **Witchery**, at the Castle end of the Royal Mile, has an authentic Scottish menu. **The Tower**, atop the Museum of Scotland, has made a name for itself with its menu of succulent Scottish seafood and wholesome steaks. The award-winning **Atrium**, attached to the Traverse Theatre on Cambridge Street, is another stylish restaurant. And down in Leith, **Martin Wishart**, on the Shore, rated two Michelin stars in his previous restaurant. His current establishment is considered by those who know to be one of Edinburgh's most delectable eating experiences.

Those with a taste for ethnic cuisine are well catered for in Edinburgh. With an abundance of Mexican, Indian, Japanese, Thai and Chinese restaurants you won't be stuck for places to sate your eastern appetites. **Britannia Spice**, on Commercial Street, close to the former Royal Yacht Britannia and Leith's Ocean Terminal, is one of the newer Indian eateries, with dishes from all over the sub-continent. Conveyor-belt sushi is purveyed at **Yo Sushi**, on Rose Street, and a somewhat more up-market version, favoured by Japanese visitors, can be sampled at **Yumi** on West Coates Street, off Haymarket Terrace. The doyen of the city's Chinese restaurants is the **Loon Fung** on Warriston Place, which has been famed for decades for its specialties: lemon chicken and crispy duck.

Outside Edinburgh, fine dining can be found at a range of country house hotels, a scattering of gastro-pubs and cheap and cheerful fish and chip restaurants. Top marks go to **Andrew Fairlie at Gleneagles**, the gourmet French restaurant of the famous hotel, presided over by Michelin-starred chef Andrew Fairlie, for his exquisite cuisine.

In Dundee you'll find a surprising number of cosmopolitan treats, but for simpler fare try the **Deep Sea**, at 81 Nethergate, which has the best fish and chips in town.

The **Agacan**, at 113 Perth Road, is a local institution, serving the best Turkish food outside Turkey and also – thanks to their policy of helping struggling artists – colourfully adorned. At **Jute**, the café-bar of Dundee Contemporary Arts, you'll find reliable bistro-style meals from lunchtime until midnight.

Glen Esk near Edzell, Angus

Dundee has a long-standing connection with Asia, which has supplied it with a plethora of Indian restaurants. The **Dil Se**, at 99-101 Perth Road, takes this tradition one step further, purveying designer Bangladeshi nosh.

The Dundee suburb of Broughty Ferry has many celebrated establishments serving a variety of foods from the world's culinary nations. **Visocchi's**, on Gray Street in Broughty Ferry, has enjoyed supplying generations of Dundee-Italian ice cream and pasta expertise. Brook Street seems an unlikely place to find a French-Moroccan bistro, but **Café Montmartre** serves up superb couscous and tagine. Another surprise is the **Ship Inn**, which is everything a traditional Scottish fisherman's pub should be, with a sensible menu that's heavy on seafood and meat. In the **Fisherman's** on Fort Street they have real ales and substantial pub lunches.

On the Anstruther seafront, the **Anstruther Fish Bar** is worth taking a detour for and in Arbroath the fish at **Peppo's** on Ladybridge Street is so fresh it's still flapping when it hits the fryer. In Perth, **Let's Eat** on Kinnoull Street, blends simplicity with sophistication and is great value for money.

Less than thirty years ago, all the pubs in Edinburgh closed at 10 pm. The city had just two discos – neither of which served alcohol. And Hogmanay was a do-it-yourself affair. Tell that to young people these days and they won't believe you. Now, Edinburgh's nightlife is legendary, with great live music venues, pubs and bars that stay open until the small hours, and clubs as good as any in Europe.

And **Hogmanay**, like the Edinburgh International Festival and its Fringe, has become a slick, dazzling, fixture on the international events calendar. In fact, Scotland's capital can claim to be Britain's only real 24-hour entertainment city, with everything from art house cinema to opera to house, garage and trance club nights.

The capital's compact layout means even the most dedicated of night owls will never get stranded in the early hours – even if there isn't a taxi when you need one (and there usually is) you're rarely more than a fifteen-minute walk from your hotel. When Edinburgh hosted the annual **MTV awards**, the channel rated the city the best ever MTV venue. In 2004, the city hosts no fewer than fourteen major international festivals and events and the almost non-stop festival calendar guarantees that there is always something happening.

The Filling Station Pub on the Royal Mile, Edinburgh

If seeking out up-and-coming-bands is your thing, head for **Bannermans** at 121 Cowgate. With frequent live music sessions, this couthy pub is also a favourite pre-clubbing

The Wheel, part of the winter wonderland in Princes Street Gardens

venue at weekends, as most of Edinburgh's favourite clubs are within walking distance.

The club scene changes fluidly, but stalwart venues include **Po Na Na**, on Frederick Street, **Gaia** on King's Stables Road, the **Liquid Room** on Victoria Street and the highly rated **Espionage**, also on Victoria Street. **Ego**, on Picardy Place, is the hub of Edinburgh's thriving gay scene, as is **C.C. Blooms**, on Greenside Place.

For a more cultured evening out, Edinburgh's theatres and concert halls stage ballet, opera, musicals and West End plays performed by local and visiting companies and ensembles. Major venues for classical music, opera, ballet and contemporary dance include the **Playhouse** and the **Festival Theatre**. The vast **Usher Hall** and the smaller **Queen's Hall** are also favourite venues for classical concerts.

Nightlife of all sorts abounds in the most unlikely venues during Festival time, when the **Assembly Rooms** become the hub of the Fringe and a must for cutting-edge stand-up comedy – book your tickets early.

Edinburgh's main theatres include the **Royal Lyceum**, an elegant Victorian building on Grindlay Street, the old **King's Theatre** on Leven Street, and contemporary venues such as the famous **Traverse**, on Cambridge Street, which continues to foster new talent and experimental drama. **Brunton Theatre**, refurbished in 1996, is home to musicals, dramas, comedy and festival events. Its resident theatre group, superb facilities and impressive productions make it a great night out. **Dance Base**, in the Grassmarket, is Scotland's national contemporary dance centre. For film lovers, the **Cameo**, in Tollcross, shows late movies, art house classics and new films. **Filmhouse** on Lothian Road shows cult movies, new releases, forgotten works and hosts the annual Film Festival.

The East's other big nightlife spot is Dundee, where the cavernous **Caird Hall** is the top venue for classical and rock concerts and claims to be the longest concert hall in Britain. When the Beatles played here in 1963 John Lennon famously asked the audience in the back row: "Can you hear me back there in Perth?" Other venues for club nights and live music include **Fat Sam's,** at 31 South Ward Rd – a local legend – and **Enigma**, also on South Ward Rd. **Fantasy Club**, on the Seagate, **Oasis,**

LISTING

BRUNTON THEATRE
Ladywell Way,
Musselburgh,
EH21 6AA
Tickets: 0131 665 2240
Fax: 0131 665 9642
www.bruntontheatre.co.uk

Brunton Theatre is easy to find, just past the bypass on the east side of Edinburgh. The theatre presents professional touring companies as well as co-productions. There is something for everyone: drama, dance, comedy, children's theatre, music, films, Fringe Festival events & pantomime.

The curling ice rink at the Letham Grange Hotel, Colliston, Angus

on St Andrews Lane, and **Oxygen,** on Brown Street, are venues on a night out.

For theatre goers, **Dundee Repertory Theatre** has a nationwide reputation and has fostered the careers of international actors as diverse as Richard Todd and Brian Cox. The home of Scotland's only full-time ensemble company, it is also the base of Scotland's leading modern dance troupe, **Scottish Dance Theatre**, and one of the UK's largest and most highly regarded community arts organisations. With the clubbing and nightlife of Dundee just thirteen miles away, St Andrews has little in the way of full-scale venues but **Ogstons**, its biggest bar, serves to keep locals, students and visitors amused.

Perth has plenty of pub-based traditional music and is one of the best places to hear real Scottish music during the annual **Accordion and Fiddle Festival** (Oct 30 2004), one of Scotland's largest folk music events. The **Perth Symphony Orchestra** provides a programme of orchestral music in the **Perth City Hall**. The city's top clubbing venue is the **Ice House,** by the river on Shore Road, a former ice store, which attracts big-name bands and DJs from London and America.

ABERDEEN

Scotland's third largest city, **Aberdeen** surfed the crest of an oil boom in the 1970s and 80s, which helped to lessen the negative impact of the decline in the North Sea fishery. With oil also on the decrease, Aberdeen is now looking around for new sources of prosperity – such as tourism. The 'Granite City', so called because of the silvery local stone used in many of its sturdy nineteenth century public buildings, has much to recommend it to the visitor.

Not only is it a convenient starting point for exploring the wild North Sea coast; but from here you can visit and enjoy the charming countryside and fishing of Royal Deeside, as well as, the wilderness of the spectacular Grampian Highlands.

Castlegate in the centre of Aberdeen

Aberdeen exhibition and conference centre

The city has its attractions too. **St Machar's Cathedral,** in the centre of Old Aberdeen – the oldest part of the city – is a solid-looking fifteenth-century building with a period-painted interior. On Union Street, the **Kirk of St Nicholas** can be dated in part from the twelfth century. **King's College,** on the High Street, is the oldest part of the **University of Aberdeen,** which was founded in 1494. Provost Ross's House, on Shiprow, contains the **Maritime Museum** with its collection of model ships and paintings. The city is also home to the fabled **Old Bridge of Dee,** a remarkable feat of sixteenth-century engineering, with its seven arches spanning the River Dee.

Arial view of Aberdeen to the harbour & docks

Strathisla distillery- dating from 1786 the oldest working distillery in Scotland

GRAMPIAN

The **Grampian Highlands** form the backbone of this picturesque region of mountains, moors, pretty river valleys and rugged coasts.

Braemar, a quaint little town on the River Dee, is one of the best locations to explore the region. From here you can walk in the barren 'pocket wilderness' of the **Cairngorm Mountains** or climb the looming 3,789 ft peak of **Lochnagar**. There are walks to suit all levels of fitness, from easy family strolls to demanding mountain hikes, which might require mountaineering skills. On the slopes of the mountain, the **Royal Lochnagar Distillery**, near Crathie, has been supplying fine malt whisky to Britain's royals since 1848. Its visitor centre tells the story of its royal connections – and lets you sample a dram or two.

Braemar also gives passage to the 'Royal Deeside', where **Balmoral Castle**, on the banks of the Dee, has been the British royal family's favourite Scottish holiday location since Queen Victoria discovered the region. The castle naturally attracts flocks of sightseers when the royals are not in residence.

There are other castles to see around the Grampian region. **Crathes Castle**, near Banchory, is an authentic medieval stronghold that has hardly been altered since it was built in 1596. **Drum Castle**, also near Banchory, is a gracious seventeenth-century manor house. Whereas in contrast, **Dunnottar Castle**, perched on a sea-crag south of Aberdeen, is a haunted shell. Built in the late fourteenth century, it was destroyed in 1715. **Castle Fraser**, at Dunecht, west of Aberdeen, was built in 1636 and is reckoned to be one of Scotland's finest examples of a baronial tower house.

Along the Grampian coast are small fishing ports such as Stonehaven and Fraserburgh, where one of Scotland's earliest lighthouses is now the **Scottish Lighthouse Museum**.

Elgin Cathedral, ruined 13th century Cathedral, Grampian

The Grampian region was once the heartland of the ancient Pictish kingdom (who vanished from history some 1,400 years ago) and even earlier, pre-Celtic civilisations. Relics of these can be seen at **Cullerlie**, where a circle of tall standing stones is believed to date from as early as 2000 BC. The **Archaeolink Prehistory Park**, near Inverurie (about 30 miles northwest of Aberdeen) is great fun, with imaginative reconstructions of Pictish life and re-enactments of Pictish battles.

HIGHLANDS

Inverness, straddling the River Ness at the head of the Moray Firth, is the eastern entryway to the northwest highlands, Scotland's remotest and most romantic region. If you are coming in from Glasgow and the west, Fort William is the most convenient stopping-off point.

The **Caledonian Canal** cuts a line through the Great Glen, linking a chain of long narrow lochs from Loch Ness in the east to Fort William in the shadow of Ben Nevis, in the west. A canal cruise through the lochs is a

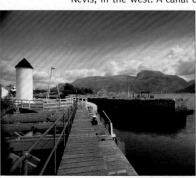

great way to see some of Scotland's most magnificent scenery, and for eager Ness fans there are 'monster hunting' cruises on **Loch Ness**.

Ben Nevis, at 4,407 ft, is a stiff hike in any weather, but there's also an easier option for the lethargic visitor, a cable car to the peak of **Aonach Mor** means you won't have to forsake the fantastic views from Britain's highest mountain.

Caledonian Canal at Corpach on Loch Eil

North of Inverness the highlands really begin and this is country that is best explored either with a hired car or on an escorted tour, as public transport is somewhat limited. From here, you can head west into the wild hills and lochs of **Torridon**, or north and east through the **Flow Country of Caithness**, a region of peat bogs and flat moorland. From Ullapool, on the west coast, you can continue round to **Cape Wrath**, or on the east coast you can head for **John O'Groats**, the northernmost point in mainland Britain.

The Ring of Brodgar between Loch of Harray and Loch of Stenness

ORKNEY

The Orkney Isles are a place apart and Orcadians feel themselves to be significantly different from mainland Scots.

Ancient stone circles testify to the earliest inhabitants of these green northern isles, but the Norsemen who settled Orkney 1,300 years ago found them unpeopled. **Mainland,** the largest island in the archipelago, is just 20 miles across and is surrounded by smaller islands – Hoy, South and North Ronaldsay, Shapinsay, Rousay, Eday, Stronsay, Sanday, Westray and Papa Westray.

Orkney's biggest town, **Kirkwall**, faces north across a sheltered inlet towards Shapinsay. Stromness, the main ferry port, faces south towards Hoy. Kirkwall's main sight is the remarkable **St Magnus Cathedral.** Built in 1137, it is named after Earl Magnus, the first Norse chief of the islands to become a Christian. Also worth seeing is the thirteenth-century **Bishop's Palace** and **Earl Patrick's Palace,** built in 1607.

Relics of even earlier times include the **Ring of Brodgar**, an enigmatic circle of thirty-six standing stones erected more than 5,000 years ago. **Unstan Chambered Tomb**, a prehistoric cairn and **Maes Howe**, a burial mound dating from around 2500 BC, are almost equally ancient and worth a visit.

SHETLAND

The remote isles of Shetland lie far out into the North
Sea and, like Orkney, were settled by Vikings around
1,200 years ago. Often wreathed in chilly sea fogs,
Shetland is best visited during the summer months, when
long, light evenings with only a couple of hours of
darkness help to compensate for its dour climate.

Lerwick, the only town of any size, is on the largest
island, called **Mainland,** and is a picturesque little port,
with a fishing harbour surrounded by stone cottages.
The **Shetland Museum,** in Lerwick, reveals evidence of
5,000 years of local history – like Orkney, Shetland is
dotted with relics of a very ancient past, from Stone Age
times and the golden age of the Picts. A seventeenth-
century stronghold, **Fort Charlotte,** guards the harbour.

Shetland's biggest attraction, however, is some 20 miles
outside Lerwick at Sumburgh Head. Archaeologists
working at the **Jarlshof** site have unearthed evidence of
a settlement from the late Stone Age (around 2000
years BC) through to the era of the Norse settlers. The
remains of Neolithic, Pictish and Viking settlements can
be seen, along with medieval farm steadings and the
manor house of the **Stewart Earls of Shetland,** who
ruled the islands from the sixteenth century.

Lerwick, the
chief town and
fishing port of
Mainland

Northern Scotland's major cities are adequately supplied with shops to meet all your requirements. Tourist hot spots such as Braemar and Ballater are choc-a-bloc with tartan kitsch for you to take home. Smaller towns in the region, however, can be disappointing for shoppers, so plan your retail therapy in Aberdeen or Inverness. In Aberdeen, the **Bon Accord Centre** is the city's main shopping mall. You'll find major name stores such as **John Lewis**, **Debenhams** and **Carphone Warehouse** in the city centre. **Union Street** and **George Street** are the Granite City's main shopping streets.

In Inverness there is the usual array of High Street names in modern shopping malls, along with smaller and quirkier shops and cafés in a cavernous and picturesque Victorian Arcade in the city centre. If you're short of holiday reading, or looking for fact or fiction of local interest **Leakey's Second Hand Bookshop** is the largest second hand bookshop in Scotland. It's housed in a former church, has shelf after shelf of books and a pleasant café-restaurant. Inverness's biggest retail mall

Albert Atreet, Mainland, Orkney

– and the largest shopping centre in the Highlands – is the modern **Eastgate Shopping Centre**, where you'll find names such as **Boots, Body Shop, Marks and Spencer, Next**, and **HMV**, along with cafés and restaurants.

Eastgate II, which opened in 2003, offers **Debenhams**, the **Gadget Shop, Laura Ashley, Monsoon** and other fashion stores and fast food restaurants.

The range of places to stay in northern Scotland includes from the comfortable to the costly, from castle hotels to a varied selection of business-oriented chain hotels in Aberdeen and Inverness, to the less expensive family-run guesthouses and bed and breakfast establishments throughout Grampian, the Highlands, and the northern isles. For budget travellers, the **Scottish Youth Hostel Association** has clean and cheerful hostels throughout the region. All of them offer affordable beds and some have twin and family rooms. In Aberdeen's West End, the **Atholl Hotel** offers quality accommodation at a price that is within reach of most budgets. Affordable accommodation in Aberdeen is also offered in the **University of Aberdeen's halls of residence** during the summer holidays. Luxury accommodation includes the **Marcliffe** at Pitfodels, on North Deeside Road, a small and personal five-star hotel. The **Old Mill Inn** on South Deeside Road offers a homely welcome at reasonable rates. **Raemoir House**, set in a 3,500 acre Deeside estate near Banchory, is ideal for a restful break. In Fort William, the **Nevis Bank Hotel** offers excellent value for money. Accommodation in the northern isles is more limited. In Kirkwall the **Albert Hotel** is recommended and in Lerwick the **Lerwick Hotel** is a choice establishment.

LISTINGS

ATHOLL HOTEL
54 King Gate,
Aberdeen, AB15 4YN
Tel. 00441224 323505
Fax 00441224 321555
Email info@atholl-aberdeen.co.uk
Web: www.atholl-aberdeen.com

Excellent privately owned hotel and popular restaurant serving fresh local produce. Large car park. Renowned for consistent and friendly service and value. Weekend breaks available from £49.50 per person per night including full Scottish Breakfast. Any Fri-Sun subject to availability. Quote RA 1.

NEVIS BANK HOTEL
Belford Road,
Fort-William,
PH33 6BY
Tel: 01397 705721
Fax: 01397 706275
Email: info@nevisbankhotel.co.uk

Ideally situated close to the centre of Fort William, and offering the very best in Highland Hospitality with attentive & friendly staff. The two Bars and Lower Falls Restaurant offers the very best in Food, Drink and atmosphere, capturing the true spirit of the Highlands.

Northern Scotland offers a surprisingly good choice of places to eat, from some of the best fish and chip shops to sophisticated country house restaurants.

Try the original **Ashvale** in Aberdeen or its branches in Elgin and Inverurie. Don't miss the **Bervie Chipper** in Inverbervie, with a second in Stonehaven (home of the deep-fried Mars Bar!). **Sandy's**, also in Stonehaven, is another good option. In Inverness, the **Castle Restaurant**, off the High Street, is one of Scotland's best traditional fry-up café-restaurants.

More expensive seafood can be found at the **Silver Darling**, beside the harbour in Aberdeen. Way up north in Scrabster, the **Captain's Galley** is the top place to eat locally-caught fresh fish while you wait for the Orkney ferry. In Fort William, the **Crannog** has great local seafood and spectacular views from its dining room at the end of a jetty on the waterfront. The finest dining in the north however is at the world-famous **Altnaharrie Inn**, across Loch Broom from Ullapool, which has eight comfortable bedrooms. The Inn is the only Michelin two-star restaurant in Scotland, and can only be accessed by boat. It is booked up months in advance, so plan well ahead.

Loch Nevis langoustines at the Old Forge pub, Inverie

Aberdeen's nightlife has been transformed by the opening of a branch of **Espionage**, Scotland's leading club chain, at 120 Union Street. With four bars on two levels and no door charge, Espionage is definitely the popular choice when it comes to after-dark entertainment in the Granite City. It's open until the early hours seven nights a week.

On level one is **Pravda**, which is usually comprised of a packed dance floor, party, pop and chart music. On level two are **Mata Hari** and **KasBar**, playing a mix of UpBeat, Rn'B and old skool. The **Frankenstein Pub**, also on Union Street, is another top venue in Aberdeen, with an extensive cocktail list and value-for-money special offers. Wait for the moment when Frankenstein's monster comes to life. Aberdeen nightlife also includes the seven-screen **Carmike Cinema Complex**, along with musicals and drama at the historic **Capitol Theatre** in the city centre. You don't go to the Scottish Highlands for Broadway-style entertainment!

'The Priory' - a nightclub in a converted church on Belmont Street, Aberdeen

Across most of northern Scotland, nightlife and entertainment focuses on bars and pubs, with frequent ceilidh evenings where you can enjoy a taste of Highland hospitality, folk music and traditional dancing. In Inverness, there's live music at **Blackfriars**, on Academy Street. If you are cruising the Caledonian Canal at Fort Augusts the **Lock Inn** ocassionally hosts live bands.

Linn of Tummel - a waterfall on the River Tummel

With so much wide-open space, Scotland is a paradise for active holidaymakers. Hill walking, mountaineering, whitewater kayaking, yachting, windsurfing, scuba diving, mountain biking and quad biking are all on offer. Gentler pursuits include golf – on some of the world's finest courses – curling, skating and angling on trout streams, lochs and offshore.

Football is of course the national obsession. Rivalry between Scotland's teams is fierce – and it's never fiercer than during a match between two teams from the same city. When Glasgow's two top teams, Celtic and Rangers go head to head, or when Edinburgh's Hearts clash with Hibernian, the excitement is palpable. That said, all regional rivalries are set aside when Scotland meets England internationally.

Rugby has a strong regional following in Edinburgh – home of **Murrayfield**, the national rugby stadium – and the Borders. For those who would rather play than watch, Scotland has superb sporting facilities – and **golf** leads the way.

It is played on scores of inexpensive local links as well as on world-famous courses such as **St Andrews** and **Musselburgh**. For lovers of the royal and ancient game, Scotland's southwest has few rivals. **Scottish Golf Southwest** opens the door to major championship venues including **Turnberry**, **Royal Troon** and **Prestwick**

The old course, St Andrews, with a view to the town beyond, Fife

Golf Club, birthplace of the Open Championship, along with nearly 100 of Scotland's best golf courses in an area of outstanding natural beauty, stretching from Gretna to the Hebrides.

Glasgow Prestwick airport is an excellent stopover to take advantage of the fine golfing country of Ayrshire. Prestwick's prestigious **St Cuthbert** and **St Nicholas'** courses start only minutes from the airport terminal and welcome visiting golfers. The **Brunston Castle Golf Club** and the **Ballochmyle Golf Club** are also conveniently near the airport. Over on the east coast, **Gullane Golf Club** offers superb greens not half an hour from Edinburgh and **Dunbar Golf Club**, on the North Sea coast, also offers a warm welcome to visitors.

Southern Scotland, with its gently rolling hills and moors, is great cycling territory. In 2004, a new venture by regional tourist boards and the Forestry Commission made the Borders and Dumfries and Galloway even more appealing to mountain bikers. The **7stanes centres**, centres of mountain biking excellence in the forests of South Scotland, offer world-class trails to suit all abilities from beginners to expert riders. With bike hire, repairs, sales and café facilities available on-site you'll be well prepared for the terrain. The centres are at **Newcastleton** and the **Tweed Valley** in the Borders and in **Kirroughtree**, **Dalbeattie**, **Glentrool**, **Mabie** and **Ae** in Dumfries and Galloway. They offer adventurous country riding, views to die for and miles of technical singletrack.

For visitors on a short break, **VisitScotland**, together with the **Perthshire Tourist Board** and some of Scotland's top adventure operators, offers **Scotland's Adventure Pass**. Value for money thrills available with the pass include a beginners' guide to surfing, complete with all the kit; kayaking or Canadian canoeing on lochs and rivers; abseiling and rock climbing; one-hour micro-light or light aircraft flying lessons; sphering and bungee jumping; canyoning, gorge walking, white water rafting and power boating.

Scotland is also hard to beat for accessible, affordable **skiing** – less than two hours from its major cities. With ski areas in the Highlands, Perthshire and Grampian including: **Nevis Range**, **Glencoe**, **Glenshee**, the **Lecht** and **CairnGorm Mountain**, all offering challenging pistes, good infrastructure and expert tuition. A short ski-break in Scotland is the perfect way to sample the delights of skiing without spending a fortune on travelling to a more costly ski destination. Check out VisitScotland's official ski site (ski.visitscotland.com) for ski packages, weather conditions, accommodation and piste maps.

Glenshee
Ski Centre,
Grampian

BALLOCHMYLE GOLF CLUB
Mauchline,
Ayrshire
Tel: 01290 550469
Fax: 01290 553657
Email:
secretary@ballochmyle.freeserve.co.uk

Situated in the heart of Burns Country, Ballochmyle Golf Club is located 12 miles from Prestwick Airport and 40 minutes from Glasgow City Centre. Playing golf on this parkland course is an ideal way to relax during visits to Scotland.

BRUNSTON CASTLE GOLF CLUB
Golf Course Road, Dailly, Girvan,
Ayrshire, KA26 9GD
Tel: +44 (0)1465 811471
Fax: +44 (0)1465 811545
Email: golf@brunstoncastle.co.uk
Web: www.brunstoncastle.co.uk

Brunston Castle Golf Course is situated in the most scenic part of Ayrshire, 5 miles from Turnberry and 20 minutes from Prestwick airport. Club Shuttle bus available for transfers. Greens open all year round. The clubhouse has full dining and bar facilities.

DUNBAR GOLF CLUB
East Links,
Dunbar, EH42 1LL
Tel: 01368 862317
Fax: 01368 865202
Email: secretary@dunbargolfclub.sol.co.uk
Web: www.dunbar-golfclub.co.uk

This Open Qualifying venue is one of the best links courses in the country. Fourteen consecutive holes run along a narrow strip of land by the Firth of Forth offering a lengthy, testing exposure to the vagaries of seaside golf.

GULLANE GOLF CLUB
Gullane, East Lothian,
EH31 2BB
Tel: 01620 842255
Fax: 01620 84 2327
Email: bookings@gullanegolfclub.com
Web: www.gullanegolfclub.com

The 3 Courses are beautifully maintained and the ball is played as it lies all the year round. The greens are as true in January as they are in July. With majestic scenery, the views stretch for 30 miles in every direction.

PRESTWICK ST CUTHBERT GOLF CLUB
East Road,
Prestwick,
Ayrshire, KA9 2SX
Tel: 01292 477101
Fax: 01292 671730
Email: secretary@stcuthbert.co.uk

Prestwick St Cuthbert Golf Club is a Parkland course of 6470 yards Par 71 within 10 minutes of the airport. This is an interesting course with several dogleg Par 4's. It has proved a popular course for outings over the years.

PRESTWICK ST NICHOLAS GOLF CLUB
Grangemuir Road, Prestwick,
Ayrshire, KA9 1SN
Contact: Mr Tom Hepburn
Tel: 01292 477608 Fax: 01292 473900
Golf Shop: 01292 473904
Established on the 3rd November 1851.

In May 1940 Henry Cotton after playing described Prestwick St Nicholas Golf Course as 'a small edition of the best championship courses we possess. The beautiful greens are made of the real stuff and are undulating to the point of being tricky and as true as billiard tables'.

4 September 2004
Braemar Gathering
Braemar, Deeside

4-5 September 2004
Edinburgh Mela
Edinburgh (various venues)

22-27 September
Merchant City Festival
Merchant City, Glasgow

8-16 October
Royal National Mod
Perth (various venues)

1-15 November
Glasgay!
Glasgow (gay club venues)

19-21 November
Fiddle
Assembly Rooms,
Edinburgh

30 Nov- 26 Dec
Capital Christmas
Edinburgh (Princes St and
various venues)

29 Dec-1 Jan 2005
Edinburgh's Hogmanay
(Royal Mile, Castle
Esplanade, the Mound)
Edinburgh

January 2005
Up Helly Aa
Lerwick, Kirkwall and other
venues in Northern Isles

12-30 January 2005
Celtic Connections
Various venues across
Scotland

17-20 March
St Anza:
Scotland's Poetry Festival
St Andrews

17 March -3 April
Glasgow International
Comedy Festival
Glasgow, various venues

2-12 April
Edinburgh International
Science Festival Edinburgh

15-18 April
Glasgow Art Fair
Glasgow

29 April-2 March
Shetland Folk Festival
Lerwick and various
venues

30 April-3 May
Spirit of Speyside
Whisky Festival
Distilleries and other
venues, Speyside

2-3 June
Download Festival,
Glasgow

3-7 June
Dundee Jazz Festival
Dundee Repertory Theatre
and other venues

3-11 June
Highland Festival
Inverness

10-13 June
Diageo Championship Golf
Gleneagles

July
Highland Games - Braemar
and other venues across
Scotland

August
Edinburgh International
Festival, Edinburgh

Edinburgh Festival Fringe
Edinburgh

Edinburgh Military Tattoo
Edinburgh

Scotland has a long and proud tradition as a centre of educational excellence. The first country in the world to introduce universal education (long before its southern neighbour), Scotland has for centuries welcomed foreign students to its colleges and universities and that tradition continues today.

Scotland's two major cities, with their concentration of university-level educational institutions, offer visiting students excellent opportunities to acquire or improve their English language skills. Scots have welcomed the benefits of their European Union membership and there is a genuinely positive and welcoming attitude to visitors from the European mainland. At the same time, many Scots feel an affinity with North America, and Scottish universities maintain close links with some of the most prestigious educational centres in the USA and Canada. All of this creates an excellent atmosphere for learning.

Cobbled high street near the university in old Aberdeen

Glasgow and Edinburgh also provide lots of scope to try out your newly acquired language skills in a lively social atmosphere. With living costs notably lower than in London and southern England, Scotland offers an affordable learning experience. Both cities have highly professional and prestigious language schools, most of them offering a full package including accommodation as well as teaching. **Global Language Services Ltd**'s team of qualified and experienced staff are readily equipped to cater for your language needs with one-to-one tuition and specially tailored programmes as part of the standard service. In central Glasgow, the **Mackintosh School of English Language**

offers a range of good-value courses, with homestay accommodation, which encourages students to use their vocabulary in conversation with their hosts. In Edinburgh's New Town, the **Randolph School of English** guarantees personal tutoring and an array of summer school courses.

LISTINGS

GLOBAL LANGUAGE SERVICES LTD
Craig House, 64 Darnley Street,
Glasgow, G41 2SQ
Tel: 0141 429 3429/3428
Fax: 0141 429 3429
Email: mail@globalglasgow.com
Web: www.globalglasgow.com

Language services consists of interpreting, translating and language tuition and with our network of interpreters, translators, tutors we are professionals in such provision. As professionals we offer a prompt, reliable and accurate provision where, when and in the manner you require.

RANDOLPH SCHOOL OF ENGLISH
63 Frederick Street,
Edinburgh, EH2 1LH
Tel: +44(0)131 226 5004
Fax:+44(0)131 226 5003
Email: randolphSE@aol.com
Web: www.randolph.org.uk

We are a small school in the centre of Edinburgh and accredited by the British Council. We offer General and Business English courses for students from all over the world, and teacher training courses (Cambridge CELTA) throughout the year.

GLOSSARY & TERMS

ENGLISH	FRENCH	GERMAN	SPANISH	ITALIAN
GREETING & PHRASES				
hello	bonjour	hallo	hola	ciao
how are you?	comment allez vous?	Wie geht es Ihnen	¿como estás	come stai?
goodbye	au revoir	auf wiedersehen	adiós	arrivederci
I like	j'aime	ich möchte	me gusta	mi piace
thank you	merci	danke	gracias	grazie
please	s'il vous plaît	bitte	per favor	per favore
DIRECTIONS				
behind	derrière	hinten	detrás	dietro
beside	à côté de	neben	al lado	accanto
help	l'aide	die Hilfe	ayuda	aiuto
in front	devant	vor	en frente	davanti a
left	à gauche	links	izquierda	a sinistra
lost?	perdu	verloren	perdido	perduto
right	à droite	rechts	derecha	destra
straight ahead	tout droit	immer geradeaus	todo recto	diritto
telephone	le téléphone	das Telefon	teléfono	telefono
ticket	le billet	die Karte	billete	biglietto
tourist office	le syndicat d'initiative	die Touristeninformation	información turística	ufficio turistico
turn	tournez	abbiegen (as in 'to turn left')	girar	girare
SITES				
castle	le château	das Schloss	castillo	castello
cathedral	la cathédrale	der Dom	catedral	cattedrale
church	l'église	die Kirche	iglesia	chiesa
library	la bibliothèque	die Bibliothek	biblioteca	biblioteca
museum	le musée	das Museum	museo	museo
statue	la statue	die Statue	estatua	statue
tour	la visite	die Tour	visita	gita
tower	la tour	der Turm	torre	torre
SHOPS AND SERVICES				
bank	la banque	die Bank	banco	banca
newsagents	le tabac-journaux	der Kiosk / das Zeitschriftengeschäft	quisco	Tabacaio/Giornalaio
pharmacy	la pharmacie	die Apotheke	farmacia	farmacia
pub	le pub	die Kneipe	pub	pub
restaurant	le restaurant	das Restaurant	restaurante	ristorante
shopping centre		das Einkaufszentrum	centro comercial	centro commerciale
supermarket	le supermarché	der Supermarkt	supermercado	supermercato
EMERGENCY				
accident	l'accident	der Unfall	accidente	incidente
assault		der Überfall	asalto	assalto
doctor	le docteur	der Arzt	médico	dottore
hospital	l'hôpital	das Krankenhaus	hospital	ospedale
injury	la blessure	die Verletzung	herida	ferita
police	la police	die Polizei	policia	polizia
thief	le voleur	der Dieb	ladrón	ladro

ENGLISH	FRENCH	GERMAN	SPANISH	ITALIAN
EATING OUT				
beer	la bière	das Bier	cerveza	birra
bill	l'addition	die Rechnung	la cuenta	conto
bread	le pain	das Brot	pan	pane
butter	le beurre	die Butter	mantequilla	burro
chicken	le poulet	das Huhn / Hühnchen	pollo	pollo
coffee	le café	der Kaffee	café	caffé
dessert	le dessert	der Nachtisch	postre	dolce
fish	le poisson	der Fisch	pescado	pesce
food	la nouriture	das Essen	comida	cibo
fruit	le fruit	das Obst	fruta	frutta
meat	la viande	das Fleisch	carne	carne
menu	le menu	das Menü	menu	menu
milk	le lait	die Milch	leche	latte
sandwich	le sandwich	das Sandwich / das belegte Brötchen	bocadillo	pannino
snack	le snack	der Imbiss	aperitivo	sputino
soup	la soupe	die Suppe	sopa	minestra
tea	le thé	der Tee	té	té
tip	le pourboire	das Trinkgeld	propina	mancia
vegetables	les légumes	das Gemüse	verdura	verdure
water	l'eau	das Wasser	agua	acqua
NUMBERS/ TIME				
hour	l'heure	die Stunde	hora	ora
minute	la minute	die Minute	minuto	minuto
second	la seconde	die Sekunde	segundo	secondo
this afternoon	cet après midi	heute Nachmittag	esta tarde	questo pomeriggio
this morning	ce matin	heute Morgen	esta mañana	questa mattina
today	aujourd'hui	heute	hoy	oggi
tomorrow	demain	Morgen	mañana	domani
yesterday	hier	gestern	ayer	ieri
one	un(e)	Eins	uno	uno
two	deux	Zwei	dos	due
three	trois	Drei	tres	tre
four	quatre	Vier	cuatro	quattro
five	cinq	Fünf	cinco	cinque
six	six	Sechs	seis	sei
seven	sept	Sieben	siete	sette
eight	huit	Acht	ocho	otto
nine	neuf	Neun	nueve	nove
ten	dix	Zehn	diez	dieci
DAYS OF THE WEEK				
Monday	lundi	Montag	lunes	lunedi
Tuesday	mardi	Dienstag	martes	martedí
Wednesday	mercredi	Mittwoch	miércoles	mercoledí
Thursday	jeudi	Donnerstag	jeuves	giovedí
Friday	vendredi	Freitag	viernes	venerdí
Saturday	samedi	Samstag	sábado	sabato
Sunday	dimanche	Sonntag	domingo	domenica

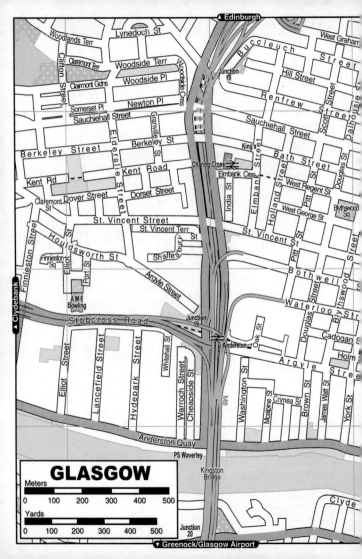

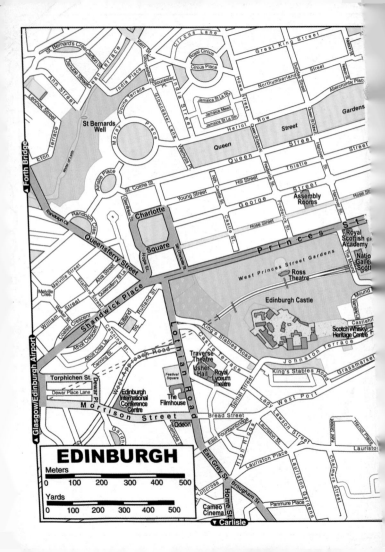